THE LISTENING CONDUCTOR

Edward-Rhys Harry

Copyright © Edward-Rhys Harry 2022
All rights reserved.
Print ISBN 9780993356705

The right of Edward-Rhys Harry to be identified as the author of this work has been asserted by him in accordance with the Copyright Designs and Patents Act 1988

No part of this publication may be reproduced, stored in a retrieval system, or transmitted in any form or by any means without the prior permission in writing of the publisher. Nor be otherwise circulated in any form or binding or cover other than that in which it is published and without a similar condition being imposed on the subsequent purchaser.

Published by
Llyfrau Cambria Books, Wales, United Kingdom.
Cambria Books is a division of
Cambria Publishing Ltd.
Discover our other books at: www.cambriabooks.co.uk

CONTENTS

About the Author	1
Foreword	5
Introduction	7
Chapter 1: Why Should We Listen?	9
Listening and Hearing	10
Listening during Choir Rehearsals	14
The Consequences of Not Listening	15
Talking	15
Not helping the voice section	17
Inaccuracy	18
Chapter 2: What Stops Us Listening?	20
Further Reasons for Listening to be Interrupted	20
How Conductors can Tell that Members of their Choir Stopped Listening	27
Chapter 3: How To Listen and What To Listen For	30
The Pre-Rehearsal Regime for Aiding Your Singer's Practice – Preparing Singers to Listen	32
How To Listen During a Rehearsal	34
How to listen during a rehearsal	36
Listening Practice Away from the Rehearsal Room	37
Listening — Rehearsal Room or Home	41
Chapter 4: Listening for ensemble	43
What is ensemble?	43
Breathing	43
The intent behind a breath	44
First syllable entries	44
Phrasing	45

Dynamics	45
Intonation	47
Blend	47
Diction and elision	48
Vowels and consonants	48
Rhythm	49
Posture	49

Chapter 5: Active listening, Exercises, Vowels and Consonants — 51

Why Should we Listen to Ourselves?	51
Six Exercises for Breath, Notes, Phrasing, Pitching, Timekeeping	51
Vowels	56
Correct Shape for — Hard Palate, Soft Palate, Teeth and Tongue	56
Consonants	58
Unvoiced Consonants	58
Voiced Consonants	59
Eliding Consonants	60
Diphthongs	62
The International Phonetic Alphabet	62

Chapter 6: Exercises for Vowels, Consonants and Diphthongs — 65

Open Vowels Placement	65
Placing Consonants	68
Practising Vowels and Consonants	76
Positioning Diphthongs	77

Chapter 7: Listening Exercises – Pairs or Small groups and the Whole Choir — 80

Pair or Small Group Exercises	80

Humming	80
Pitching and Rhythm	81
Scalic Work	81
Lip Syncing	82
Listening and Syncing with Closed Eyes	82
Back-to-Back	82
Whole Choir Exercises	83
Silence	83
Dynamic Isolation	84
Quartets	85
Mirrored Vowels	85
Posture	86
'Ear' Training	86
Take the Conductor Away	87
Lights Out	87
Chapter 8: Exercises: General, Elision, Listening	**88**
General	88
Elision	93
Listening	96
Chapter 9: Blending	**100**
Why Does a Choir Need to Blend?	100
Helping Your Choir to blend	101
Non-Blenders: An Approach	103
Blending Exercises	104
Voice Types	104
What is Voice Placement?	106
Voice Types	109
Chapter 10: Exercises — Blending, Rhythm, Syllabic Placement	**114**

Blending	114
Rhythm	119
Syllables	122

Chapter 11: Listening to Create Vocal Colours — 125

Light and Dark	126
The Effect of the Moving Parts	126
Twang	127
Vocal Colour Exercises	131

Chapter 12: Vocal Health & Development: Listening for Vocal Changes — 135

General Overuse of the Voice	135
The Vocal Cords	137
Vocal Cord Disorders	137
Changing Voices - Cambiata	140
More Serious Medical Issues	141
Ageing	141
A Note on Vocal Warmups	143

Chapter 13: Listening to Feedback — 146

Listening to Feedback: Singer to Singer	146
Listening to Feedback:	147
Groundswell: Listening to Strong Opinions	149
Managing the Management:	151
Listening to Working Groups	152

Chapter 14: Criticism — 154

Personal or private feedback: unwanted advice	154
Listening to Criticism: A Root Map	155
Self-Preservation whilst Listening	157
Handling Criticism the Right Way	158
Listening to Audience Feedback	160

Listening to Feedback from Sponsors or Event Organisers   161
Asking for Input   162
Basic Feedback Chart   163

Chapter 15: Listening in a Post-Pandemic World   **164**
What am I listening for or what might I observe?   167
How do I manage the symptoms?   168
New Ideas   169
Who Can I Call upon for Help and Support?   170

Chapter 16: Heart, Soul, and Breath: Listening for Intent   **171**
What Do We Mean by Intent?   171
How can we Identify Singing and Conducting with Intent?   173
What Stops our Intention to Sing and to Listen?   174
Why Should Singers Listen and Sing with Intent?   175
The Three Principles of Embodiment: Heart, Soul, Breath   176
Matching Intent with Direction   177
A Note about the Intent of Your Breath   178

Chapter 17. Connections   **179**
The Conductor's Connection   181
About Public Performances   183

Chapter 18: In a Nutshell   **186**
Listening: A Discipline   186
Listening: A Practised Art   187
Listening: A Necessity   188
Listening: A Courtesy   189
Listening: A Tool   189

Resources   **191**
Bibliography   **192**

About the Author

Edward-Rhys Harry is a conductor who has over 25 years' experience of directing singing ensembles and singing workshops in educational, community and professional contexts. He has directed singing festivals in many countries across the globe and believes passionately that singing in choirs can and does change lives for the better. He is director of Coro Optimum Ltd., a training, support, and mentoring programme for conductors of all ages and remains in demand as a choral conductor and clinician.

For several years, he was Artistic Director of Llangollen International Musical Eisteddfod. He holds undergraduate and postgraduate degrees from the University of Bangor, (BMus(hons)/PGDip.Mus.Tech) University of West London (LCM) (MMus Composition), Royal Welsh College of Music and Drama (MA Choral Conducting) and his PhD was in composition at the University of Aberdeen. Whilst at RWCMD, he was awarded the Laura Ashley Fellowship Award and the Glynne Jones Scholarship Award for Choral Conducting, each consecutive year; at Aberdeen he was the recipient of an Elphinstone Scholarship in music as well as the Derek Ogston Fellowship Award in Composition.

He is Principal Conductor and Musical Director of London Welsh Male Voice Choir, Musical Director of Harlow Chorus, London Welsh Chorale, Chamber Choir Wales, and Artistic Director of The Harry Ensemble (www.harryensemble.com).

His composition and arrangement catalogue is published by Universal Edition (Vienna), Boosey & Hawkes, Novello, (London), Banks Music Publishing Ltd., (York), Chichester Music Press (Hampshire) and Curiad Cyf.(Wales).

Dr Harry is a member of the Royal Society of Musicians and a Fellow of the Royal Society of the Arts. In 2021 he was awarded the Glanville Jones Award for Outstanding Contribution to Music in Wales by the Welsh Music Guild. He is the representative for Wales on the board of directors and trustees of the UK's largest leisure time community, Making Music. He is represented by Val Withams at Choral Connections: www.choralconnections.com.

For further information: www.edwardrhysharry.com

Acknowledgements

This book would not have been possible without the input of several supportive and encouraging colleagues, friends, and family to whom I owe a huge debt of thanks.

When I received my education in choral conducting, through a scholarship to the Royal Welsh College of Music and Drama, I was introduced to a group of mentors who have since become brilliant colleagues. In fact, their collective and incredibly inspiring teaching is one of the reasons that I have always wanted to contribute to choral literature. It was to this first group of people I turned to, for feedback on the early manuscript of *The Listening Conductor*. My thanks, therefore, to Adrian Partington (*BBC National Orchestral/Chorus of Wales and Director of Music at Gloucester Cathedral*) for his detailed input on form and order, my thanks also to Neil Ferris (*BBC Symphony Chorus*) for his challenging thoughts on revising some of the angles and for encouraging me to be bolder in addressing the audience for whom I wanted to write.

Lucy Hollins (*AMD University of Warwick, Associate Conductor London Symphony Chorus, Principal Guest Conductor for Cambridge Philharmonic*) was responsible for teaching me how to direct youth choirs without words – an incredible practitioner who unlocked a new passion for teaching and mentoring in me, who I now class as a valuable friend, provided me with insightful and sensitively wise extended thoughts on several subject areas covered across multiple chapters.

My other mentor at RWCMD was Prof. Simon Halsey CBE (City of Birmingham Symphony Orchestra & Chorus and Director of the Choruses at London Symphony Orchestra, Professor and Director of Choral Activities, University of Birmingham) who made sure I did not write myself into a corner at the very beginning (much like he made sure I didn't conduct myself into a corner in term 1 at RWCMD!) and ensured that I kept close to explanatory points without becoming overly wordy. His support and encouragement were so inspiring during the writing for this project. As you will see, he also, very kindly, agreed to write the foreword to this book and for that I am very grateful. All these amazing practitioners helped me with the same positive attitude and always encouraged me to keep going or expand what I wanted to say. If you get the chance to work with those I mention above, please do it, they will surely help shape and develop your directing careers as they absolutely did mine.

When one creates a manuscript for a book, it is possible to become so involved with what one wishes to say that keeping an editor's eye on the whole manuscript is not easy. Edda Hendry has acted as editor on this manuscript and has been an excellent colleague to work with; her insight has proved to be important for the layout and logic of the book and I am grateful to her for her assistance, support, and enthusiastic encouragement.

In the same way, I am delighted to be published by Cambria Books and for their CEO, Chris Jones' faith in the book in all its formats. I am also grateful to Adam Hathaway at Hathagraphics Ltd., for the design artwork and illustrations, which helped augment the project so well.

This book - and its companion podcast - came about following several intense but inspiring workshops and rehearsals with two choirs either in between or just after the COVID-19 pandemic: the London Welsh Chorale (www.londonwelshchorale.org.uk) and The Harry Ensemble (www.harryensemble.com).

My thanks to both choirs for their input to this book either knowingly or unknowingly! It is a pleasure and honour to direct them and watch them develop so earnestly; my thanks therefore to Ruth Brooks, LWC chair and all on the managing committee there (and the faithful members of 'The Chorale' itself), and to the board of directors at The Harry Ensemble – Carolyn Lewis, Clare Bayman and Maggi Ratcliffe - and the dedicated singers who have performed countless overseas premieres with me in many countries.

Finally, I'd like to thank my family for their continued support and patience in my endeavours. I am more grateful for them than they will ever know: my mother, Marilyn, my brothers, Simon and Owen, my sister-in-law Nicola and my cherished nieces, Jessica, and Sophie.

Foreword

I am thrilled with this book by my colleague Edward-Rhys Harry. It is full of great tips from a conductor experienced with choirs of all types.

We all need stimulation and this book, written with an engagingly light touch, will help conductors, singers and choir administrators stay fresh.

There is never a day on which we are not challenged by new problems and it's good to know that we, members of the enormous worldwide family of choral musicians, can turn to each other for advice and solace.

Simon Halsey
Cologne
March 2022

"...singleness of sound begins with the listening..."
-Robert Shaw 1991

Introduction

The uncomfortable silence ensued. How long had it been now?!

Seated in front of the singers, I looked out to them, unable to find words to start addressing some of the things that were stopping the choir from sounding better.
  I put my head down in the score, as if the answers were somehow lurking in there, waiting to be discovered, like hidden treasures in an archaeological dig.
  What should I say? What was I going to do with a group of 120 singers in front of me wanting to rehearse, wanting to improve, and wanting to create music? What should I have been looking for? Where should I begin? How should I begin? How could I make things better? The members of the choir began to get restless, mumbling to themselves.
  "OK," I managed, finally, 'let's sing it again!"

This was me, many years ago, standing in front of a large community chorus, putting a concert of music together that would eventually tour the North West of the UK. It was generally successful — but more by chance than anything else. I had studied and graduated from a music degree and thought I knew how to conduct choirs. Suddenly the reality seemed like a different job altogether. I know now that the first thing I should have done was to listen.

Of all the skills needed to sing in or direct a group of singers of any size, listening is one of the most important. Too often the assumption of aspiring conductors is that waving your arms around at the front will be enough to make a choir work. Too often those who enjoy singing in choirs get caught up in remembering which note, rhythm or word comes next in the music in a performance, rather than being in the happy position of knowing the music well enough to understand how to interact with others in an ensemble.

The Listening Conductor discusses one of the most important but least mentioned parts of choral activity: the power of listening. It can transform rehearsals, musical relationships and public performances by developing sensitivity, familiarity, a better interpretation of the music and embraces the sheer humanity of making music together with our voices.

Written as a handbook for choral conductors who work with singing groups of any size or age, *The Listening Conductor* provides thoughts and observations on how listening skills can be interpolated into warm-up exercises or any choral repertoire to help choirs and their directors develop their own unique sound through the consistent application of listening. It challenges conductors to re-think their approach to listening and to reap the rewards from doing so. It lays out the foundation of listening as the core discipline needed for a successful choir and asks the question 'what should we listen for?'

If you direct a group of singers, this book is for you. The hope is that it will bring you musical freedom of expression and allow you to enjoy making music in an even more productive and powerful way.

Chapter 1: Why Should We Listen?

Throughout our lives, listening is one of the basic principles that aid our learning. Growing up, we listened to the warnings of our parents or carers, being told for example, not to cross the road without looking left and right first, or not to touch the hot oven in the kitchen or to hold someone's hand if the steps ahead were too steep.

As we grew older though and gained some understanding, we may have gone through a period where we thought we were mature enough to stop listening to others and to make decisions for ourselves. Typically, when it comes to choosing a boyfriend or girlfriend, flat or housemates, a college or university subject choice or a career path, avoiding the advice of those who believe that they know us better than we do ourselves. Part of life's learning for all of us is how to manage our decisions and balance listening to the advice (wanted or unwanted!) from others as we go along. More on advice taking later!

The thing is, we can often take listening — or perhaps more commonly, *not* listening — for granted. *Not* listening is a skill we develop in life and one we can have quite a high level of ability in!

As members of a choir or as someone who leads a choir, listening is paramount. Without listening, a choir simply cannot function. Being involved with a choir, whether it is your local choral society, Church choir or a large philharmonic chorus that travels the world, is a wonderful opportunity to make friends, reap the health benefits (physical and mental) of singing together and enjoy a hobby or career that can be both educational and bring you a personal sense of satisfaction and achievement as you finally learn to sing that particularly difficult section of Brahms' music correctly or take part in a performance of a standard that goes past what you originally thought was achievable.

But this opportunity to take part or direct choirs will not work unless you are able to listen. And I don't mean just to hear what is going on around you, but to fully listen and learn from that listening.

We must, therefore, undo the years we may have spent not listening so we can develop proper choral listening skills which contribute to a better experience, as leaders or singers.

Listening and Hearing

Listening and hearing are two different things. They are two different words with different meanings and outcomes. When I'm working with choirs in workshops or rehearsals, I often reference the Merriam-Webster dictionary entries on hearing and listening:

Hearing: "…the process, function, or power of perceiving sound; specifically: the special sense by which noises and tones are received as stimuli."

Listening: "…to pay attention to sound; to hear something with thoughtful attention; and to give consideration."

If you hear an ambulance siren or the horn of a car, you are being alerted that all may not be well somewhere or with someone. You can hear unwanted chatter whilst watching a film in a cinema or hear the irritating sound of someone unwrapping a noisy sweet wrapper whilst you are trying to listen to a soloist singing your favourite operatic aria in a concert performance.

In the scenarios just mentioned, your hearing is unpleasantly distracted by a particular noise. Pleasant distractions might include hearing the 'hum' of a new city or the sound of crickets late at night while on holiday — different sounds from what you are used to 'back home'. On hearing different background sounds, we may choose to listen to them for a short while and then allow them to fade into the background of our hearing periphery, as we get used to them being there.

I have always found the relationship between hearing and listening to be a fascinating one because - on the surface - they seem to be similar in meaning, when, in fact, hearing is the more passive activity and listening the proactive activity of the two.

Workplace training today often raises the difference between hearing and listening, as part of developing emotional intelligence to aid good business decision-making. A typical two-step plan (for good listening) in the business world often looks like this:

- Focus on the other person (and not on yourself) – keep eye contact, stop all unnecessary other activity, put your own opinions to one side momentarily
- Try to gain confirmation of what you have just heard by repeating back what you believe the other person has said. Do this using different but similar wording, to reflect the same point of view they have just made

In fact, poor listening is fast becoming an identifiable factor in poor management, in the world of work. This is because poor listening can lead to wrong assumptions and misunderstandings, **or** misinterpretations that can really affect a business, a department, or a client relationship.

Why listen?

Directing choirs is not strictly or exclusively about beating patterns.

Don't misunderstand, we need beating patterns to help us differentiate between beats in a bar and choral singers need beats to help them sing together and to be able to engage with a pulse. Singers also need to be able to clearly understand 'what the other hand is doing' – identifying dynamics, crescendo and decrescendo, phrasing gestures, articulative gesture, gestures relating to the intent of making music and breathing – the hand that is not conducting the beats communicates a cornucopia of interpretation; interpretation does not have to be limited to one hand either. This means that conducting singers successfully is not about singing along and waving your arms in the air.

It is easy for conductors to become very concerned with how to beat or how to conduct passages of music. It's necessary that conductors should learn and rehearse the technical aspects of directing the music, but this is better done in front of a mirror at home or with a conducting coach, than brought to the rehearsal room. By the time a conductor gets to the rehearsal room they should be rehearsed and 'ready to go': they should know where the breathing should be, how the phrasing should be shaped, how the dynamics work, where the vocal 'pitfalls' lie (and what questions the singers may ask in this regard), how the syllables, elision, diphthongs, vowels and consonants should sound, where the tempi can be manipulated to fit the forecast end of a breath, where the balance of voices may change, where the challenging intervals or harmonic changes are – there is more but hopefully this clarifies that conductors work hard away from the rehearsal room in order to be ready for what the rehearsal room presents in a session. Effective conductors arrive to rehearse and have prepared; ineffective conductors arrive at a rehearsal 'hoping for the best'.

Why?

Because conductors will not know, notice, understand, foresee, or hear what happens in the rehearsal room if they are not already at a point – from rehearsal number 1 – where they know their job enough to be able to *listen* to the ensemble of singers they are leading.

It's worth remembering that if conductors have done their preparatory work before the rehearsal and they feel more than adequately prepared to lead others in creating the music they have been preparing, then they will have reached the freedom point I have previously mentioned. A roomful of singers must assume that the reason a conductor is standing before them is because they know what they are doing – because they have prepared – and so entrust their voices and music making into the hands of the person leading.

The person leading needs to be available (and not distracted) to listen to the output and efforts of those singing for several reasons:

- To assess
- To help fix
- To help refine
- To engage

The last point is as important as the others. We cannot hope to engage with those we are leading if we are troubled by not being prepared enough. We owe it to those who have committed to preparing, rehearsing, and performing music in a vocal ensemble, to be as ready for the task in hand as we have asked those singing to be. In any other job if one was given a task to do one would ensure it was done to the best of one's ability and the same should be said for musicianship, whether performing or directing. Our ears need to be engaged so that we can help, support, direct and encourage the singers in a choir to perform at their best.

Listening, as a director, is perhaps the most important courtesy we should afford the singers we lead.

Listening and Hearing

As conductors we carry the dual responsibility of listening to the voices we are directing and hearing the outcome of their singing together.

When I **listen** to a choir I listen so that:

- I engage musically with them and involve myself with the same act of music making as I direct the singing
- I can assess the ensemble quality
- I listen for individual voices, 'leading' voices, unevenly blended sections
- I listen to small groups of voices or individuals, or rows of singers, to assess the current learning at hand, to gain information on what sections of music need to be rehearsed again and to assess confidence levels
- I listen to assess general progress in rehearsals

When I **hear** a choir as I rehearse and direct, I:

- Hear music being made by a vocal ensemble
- Might hear general 'blemishes', errors, or a lack of confidence
- Might hear moments of inaccuracy that draw my attention
- Might hear occasions in the performance or rehearsal that I know are not fully correct, but I can't ascertain why without delving into a score and needing time to work it out
- May not hear issues with tempo and ensemble
- May not hear inaccurate intervals being learned

Listening during Choir Rehearsals

There are several important reasons as to why we should be listening during a choir rehearsal. In fact, leading a choir should primarily be all about listening and then reacting or responding to what has been heard.

At the beginning of a choral rehearsal or workshop, a good leader will ensure that there are warmup exercises to help us 'warm up' our singing voices that engage the entire vocal mechanism and breath support necessary to sing well — a quick 'refocus' on the physical requirements or demands on our bodies for singing.

Warmup exercises also serve as a refocus on what it means to listen.

A warmup may begin with all present singing the same exercise. Where does the pitch come from so that we all start singing on the same musical note: a piano, a pitch pipe, a tuning fork, the voice of the leader? How do we all know which note to start singing from? We listen for it.

And when we listen for it and hear it, we can act upon it – together.

We need to listen for it and so we do. We may even confirm that we've heard the starting pitch correctly, by humming it back to ourselves subconsciously, so that we can listen to the note in our bodies, hear how it sounds and compare it to the pitch of others. Basic behaviour that we learned from a very early age: 'call and response'.

In a choral rehearsal the 'call and response', triggered by listening to musical pitches has become habitual for a complex set of behaviours:

- Listen
- Confirm the pitch given to us by repeating it in our own bodies
- Correct if necessary
- Confirm the first musical pitch needed for singing is now set in our hearing and pitching
- Begin singing with that first pitch when directed to do so

And so, the basic principle required for a successful rehearsal is placed immediately before us in its total transparency: listening.

The art of listening takes practice and is a discipline that can be developed – should be developed — by all members of a choir, anyone accompanying a choir and anyone leading a choir. There can be any number of distractions in and outside of a rehearsal room that can detract from your listening. From my observations, some of these are:

- Electronic devices (such as a mobile phone) making a noise
- Emergency vehicle sirens or other vehicles
- Road works and maintenance
- Fire or Car alarms
- Other groups rehearsing in the same building
- The person next to you talking (to you or someone else)
- The sound of your own voice should it make an unexpected or unwanted sound or 'sound out of tune'

All the above noises can happen regularly, but it is our choice to expect them and not let them detract attention or allow them to be a welcome distraction.

It sounds pedantic to suggest that we might prepare ourselves for such extraneous noises and to hear them but not listen to them and thus become distracted — but this should be our aim.

The Consequences of Not Listening

Not listening during a rehearsal has several consequences. Later we will discuss the potential repercussions of not listening as a director of a choir but for now we will discuss what happens if singers fail to listen or stop listening, when singing as part of an ensemble.

Talking

I don't know about you, but I consider the social aspect of singing in a choir to be as important as the singing and performing itself. Indeed, lifelong friendships, relationships, marriages and children have been born from belonging to choirs so they can be an important part of a person's life.

It is important to learn how to balance the social aspects of rehearsing together, whether you are a professional or an amateur. Talking to others — friends and colleagues in a choir — is a natural thing to do. You want to share your enjoyment (or the opposite!) of a particular passage or movement, or suddenly remember to ask a friend a question. The problem however, is *the loss of instructions from the conductor*. It is not unusual for a conductor to have to repeat instructions, more than twice, so that everyone has heard them, marked them in their scores and is ready to 'rehearse them in' to their performance. Talking can be a major distraction and a conversation between two people may distract a group of more than 5 or 6 people enough so that musical directions must be repeated. The efficiency of a rehearsal is thus disrupted, along with the general pace and flow of a rehearsal. Therefore, general conversation with friends and colleagues needs to wait until the break or end of rehearsal.

However, time should be allowed for rehearsal-related questions. Singers may not always feel 'ready' for a performance or may not remember the musical instructions for interpreting a certain section. Conductors may therefore ask singers to write down any queries on a separate note pad and raise these topics at an acknowledged 'pause point' in the rehearsal. This is a positive way of communicating, allowing room for questions or discussions but instituted at a time convenient to the conductor. It's good rehearsal and member management.

Singers are not always aware that some conductors have razor-sharp hearing and can hear conversations from a long way away, even from the other side of a room; often these conversations start with a query to a friend or neighbour. Conductors should try not to be distracted by these small conversations or must learn how to stop them by addressing distracting talk with a general question like, 'Sopranos are you ready?' This will help quieten conversations quickly and effectively, whilst re-addressing the need to focus on the rehearsal; it may also raise an important query that will need clarifying so that the singer asking is no longer distracted by needing an answer.

Headline advice for talking:

- To manage the social aspects of choir rehearsals and to minimise any distraction by members talking to each other, the conductor needs to introduce definite, regular rehearsal breaks
- Suggest that singers use a separate notepad to write down questions relating to the music and rehearsal, or, even things

they want to chat with friends and colleagues about, for raising them at a later time.

Not helping the voice section

Another important outcome of not listening lies within performing and singing together itself: singers who do not listen to those around them may be singing in an isolated way, which may become 'out of step' or 'not in sync' with their voice sections.

Voice sections should sing together and sound together. They are a subset of the whole of the choir; choirs are usually made up of more than one voice section. When someone belongs to a voice section, they belong to the smaller team of people that help make the choir a whole entity, who sing together.

Not listening to the other voices in the same voice section does have consequences. Here are some of them:

- A singer's voice may not be at the same dynamic or volume as others around them and so will 'stick out' and sound 'individual'. This has the knock-on effect of making the general sound from that voice section uneven
- If a singer's ears are 'in tune' with their voice section they will learn when and how to breathe together, be sensitive to placing consonants together (clearly and simultaneously) and will sing with the same shaped mouths when singing vowels. Singers will also become aware and more sensitive to when these things are not quite right, enabling them to either discuss this with their voice section or to raise it with the person who is leading the rehearsal, or self-correct as necessary
- Not listening to your voice section may mean that singers' vocal entries are too early or too late and so the 'general sound' of the voice section may be 'ragged' or 'untidy'

Therefore, committing to becoming part of the unique sound of a voice section and therefore the choir, starts with a singer's ability to listen to others and then blend their voice together with others as the voice section works 'as one'.

Headline advice for singers in a voice section:

- Listen to each other and learn to blend your singing together so that you are 'in sync'
- Don't rely on another voice or try to 'lead' with your own voice

There are occasions where singers may feel that they know a section of music well and so to 'help' their voice section, they choose to sing louder than everyone else, in order to help 'lead' the learning. Whilst this is commendable behaviour, it does, in fact, not help for these reasons:

- The voice section becomes 'reliant' on hearing that one voice, which distracts them from listening to the choir as a whole and may even distract them from following the beat or direction of the conductor
- The 'leading' singer will become vocally tired of 'leading' and may cause themselves vocal fatigue or vocal damage as a result of 'over-singing'

Inaccuracy

Not listening carefully can mean that singers end up learning sections of music or phrases - or even text - that are inaccurate. If they allow themselves to continually rehearse these incorrectly, the inaccuracies may become so 'entrenched' in their singing and muscle memory that they will find it very difficult to 'unlearn' what they have been doing. Specifically, the casualties of not listening carefully that I am addressing here are:

- Incorrect rhythm
- Inaccurately pitched intervals
- Singing the wrong text or adding an extra letter such as an 's' on to the end of a word
- Singing an entirely different section to everyone else because the singer didn't listen to the instructions from the conductor

Fortunately, these can be corrected or wholly avoided by listening carefully and ensuring that singers learn accurately from as early in the rehearsal process as possible.

Headline advice for inaccuracy:

- Always be on your guard for singers sounding differently to the others around them. Be quick to analyse why and don't be afraid to ask to listen to sections where you listen and find 'rogue' singers
- Keep your ears open for which sections are being rehearsed
- If rehearsing another voice section, ask the other singers to attempt to rehearse their own part alongside, in their head or by humming their notes (this will stop them talking and help with their learning).

We have now discussed why we should listen and what the consequences are if we don't listen. Generally, rehearsals are interrupted by a lack of concentration as a direct result of not listening. Everyone wants the best for their choir, to perform to the highest standard possible, to enjoy singing together, to make music together and to feel a sense of achievement and kinship whilst doing so. Listening whilst rehearsing is the greatest skill we can bring to enhance all choir activities.

Chapter 2: What Stops Us Listening?

There are many things that can stop us from listening during a rehearsal. For example, many of us will recall hazy summer terms in school when we stared out of the window wishing we were outside rather than 'stuck in a classroom'. The seeds of what distracts us as adults are sown early.

In the previous chapter I set out a list of extraneous things that stop us listening (e.g., electronic devices, sirens and fire alarms). However, there are other causes that stop us from listening. I wonder if any of the following will resonate with you?

Further Reasons for Listening to be Interrupted

"What is happening in my life..?"

All of us have thoughts and cares and concerns in our private lives that we simply cannot help swirling around in our minds – particularly as we open ourselves up to an artistic and expressionistic activity such as singing. Singing solo or in a group requires us to 'get in touch' with our sensitive side and 'unlock' an expressive, emotive side to our personalities. This in turn helps us to relax and may also allow us to 'let out' emotion as we sing – one of the good reasons to join a choir in the first place. As singers internally attune to their choir with whom they sing, relax and learn to express themselves through their singing, their minds also relax. This can sometimes have the effect of thoughts or concerns suddenly being remembered or magnified, which in turn become a distraction and stop us from listening. I am sure we can all identify with this reason.

Singers should be encouraged to expect and then manage this most personal of distractions – as I said previously, singing in a choir is not only good for the body, but also the mind. My only advice to combat distractions like these is to ask singers to remember that joining a choir is 'you time': singers give up their time to join with a choir as an activity that they enjoy, whether they are paid to do it or not, and so they should treat their rehearsal time as precious; it is a time for them to improve at what they do along with a group of like-minded people, all striving for the best outcome possible. It's OK to treat rehearsals as sacrosanct – singers are invested in them and should try not to allow 'outside influences' to distract them from the activity they love. In short, try to shut it all out, if possible!

"I don't like this!"

It is amazing how distracting and sometimes off-putting, opinions on a piece of music can become. There is nothing more disappointing than to be presented with a new piece of music and to learn that it isn't liked. A choir member may feel 'let down' by the experience and somewhat 'put off' by it. It might deter them from wanting to learn it, so they do not prioritise it. When the time comes to rehearse it together they will not have spent much of their own time trying to learn it outside of the rehearsal room. As a conductor, you may have to rehearse and perform music that you dislike but it might influence how much you prepare for it or how much energy you invest in the rehearsal itself. To combat this, let's remember:

- All music must be rehearsed and prepared adequately for it to be performed well
- Good members of a choir and good conductors will learn to disregard their own personal feelings for a piece of music, *for the good of the whole choir*
- Remember, negativity breeds distraction and stops listening

This last point is very important. Your own personal negativity toward a piece, if not put aside, may lead to further negativities surfacing and is bound to close your mind to the music in question. As a result, distractions - physical or mental - are welcomed when the music is being rehearsed, which in turn compounds your feelings of negativity associated with the music in question. This in turn might lead to an unhappy feeling and minor dread for that part of the rehearsal.

At the very least, your dislike of a piece of music will stop you *listening* to it, at the worst, singers may not want to attend the rehearsal.

"Er...I haven't learned this yet,"

Being unfamiliar with a piece of choral music that you are trying to sing stops you listening to the whole choir. This is normal and acceptable when presented with a piece of music that a singer is seeing for the first time; they will need to 'sight-read' their way through it and that requires concentration on this activity only. As the piece becomes more regularly rehearsed though, it is important that singers learn their vocal part as quickly as possible, so that unfamiliarity can be dispensed with. It is only when they know their part with confidence that they can really enjoy singing it and can enjoy listening to it working with the other vocal parts, enabling them to contribute freely to the whole. If they are a singer who does not read music easily, it will be important that they support the development of their voice section by:

- Finding out if there are 'learning aids' for their voice part available either online or in retail stores
- Finding out if any members of their voice section get together outside of the usual rehearsal times to rehearse and learn together; if they don't, see if you can make it happen!
- If none of the above is possible, simply spending time reading through their music, becoming familiar with the text, sections or movements, the performance directions printed in the score and their notes from rehearsals will help to speed up the learning process

Whichever method a singer chooses, remember that the aim is to free your singers from the shackles of unfamiliarity. There can be nothing worse than feeling ill-prepared or under-confident about the music you are about to perform. Not feeling confident or happy means that singers will not fully enjoy or appreciate performing the music to an audience — and could even lead to mistakes being made.

"Pardon?"

Conductors see many things. It is worth noting that. Good conductors can tell if members of a choir have had a bad day, are singing well, need to go over something, are unfamiliar with something or if something distracting is on their mind. They can also tell if a singer is uninterested in what is happening in the rehearsal room.

Lack of interest is a real rehearsal killer and can be quite distracting for a conductor. Imagine seeing one very grumpy looking face in a sea of those trying hard to rehearse and learn together. Easy to spot — as you can imagine.

It is, of course, difficult for a singer to manage too. If a singer is just not interested in what is happening in the rehearsal, they will almost certainly not listen. After a rehearsal, singers should be encouraged to ask themselves, "What did I get out of the rehearsal today?" If the answer is "…not much.", they may have to ask themselves wider questions and should realise that being disinterested shows. Distraction can become 'infectious', putting other singers at risk, but more importantly, disinterest directly impacts on being able to listen.

"Another pint please… are these sandwiches for us?"

There are two points to be made here. Let's start with food: eating is a very important thing we must all do so that we have energy and stay alive. Unfortunately, certain foods can stick to the inside of the mouth or throat. It is wise therefore to eat well before, or after a scheduled rehearsal. Why am I saying such an obvious thing? Because feeling hungry and lack of energy are distractions enough to stop any one of us from listening in a rehearsal. Singing is an activity that requires attention and focus and no one wants to be distracted by a rumbling tummy.

The other point here is alcohol. You will be aware that consuming alcohol has a relaxing effect, but did you know that it can affect the small hair cells that receive the sounds we hear which, in turn, translate them to our brains for understanding? As a result, drinking alcohol either before or during a rehearsal can have a temporary effect on our listening. Alongside this, alcohol can also affect memory. Singers should not allow alcohol to impair their listening or their memory. Consuming alcohol before a concert may help to calm or depress the nervous system, but it can also lead to temporary memory loss, lessened concentration and slurred speech. The loss of the 'fight or flight' adrenaline, which is needed for concentration, may lead to the possibility of 'errors' in performance. In short, alcohol is best consumed *after* a rehearsal or concert, as it will impair a singer's concentration and listening.

"I just wanted to let you know…"

There is no doubt that common illnesses such as coughs and colds are unpleasant to manage but we cannot escape them. Recent times have seen the world dealing with a global COVID-19 pandemic, bringing health and safety in groups, particularly choirs, 'under the microscope'.

If a singer shows symptoms of a viral infection, they should be advised not to attend the rehearsal. An unwell singer will not be in the right frame of mind to listen and concentrate on the rehearsal. Besides which, should they choose to attend a rehearsal and take their illness with them, the chances are that they will share that illness with others before too long; as whichever viral infection they are carrying will spread first throughout their voice section and then on to others, as well as to the conductor and accompanist. This may then impact rehearsals for weeks to come as numbers of those in attendance vary due to the mini 'choir epidemic' that may have been started by that one singer. In short, if you are feeling unwell, it's OK to stay at home and this is what you should do.

"Well, I don't agree with that."

One final distraction is another of a personal nature: our thoughts on who is singing or accompanying. When I say thoughts, I mean opinions on how they are dressed, in which manner they are contributing to the choir, whether they look well, whether they have put on or lost weight, that stain on their jacket pocket, whether they are wearing new glasses, etc. You can see how easy it is for these sorts of thoughts to become distractions, can't you?

The other aspect of this is whether you like or dislike an individual in the first place. If you dislike someone, the chances are you may be waiting for an opportunity— something you disapprove of — to tell them so. The reverse of this is wanting to support them so much that you are too busy smiling and nodding your head to listen to what they are singing in the first place. All these things can stop us from listening to the sound of the choir as a whole. It can be difficult to disassociate yourself from personal thoughts and feelings about those singing, but we must all aspire to deal with them away from the rehearsal room – to not let them impair our function as leaders.

What stops you listening as a conductor?

As I've previously mentioned there are many things that can stop us listening but as directors of choirs the biggest of these is not knowing the music. Put simply, we must be fully prepared before a rehearsal so that we can listen, identify the areas that need attention and tend to them, whether working with an amateur or professional chorus. When I describe 'not knowing the music' I mean that we have not studied the score, not analysed the structure of the music, not sought to understand the composers' intentions, not listened to recordings, not rehearsed the beating patterns, don't know it well enough to be able to sing through sections alone or 'hear it internally'.

What trips us up in the rehearsal room is unfamiliarity with the landscape of the music with which we are working. We must know the music. Too much relies upon us being free to listen. The rehearsal room is not the place to be pondering tempi or articulation, we should know these things.

If we are listening to the choir we are directing, it is obvious to them and they respond to this. Basic human engagement – you communicate, I listen, then I communicate, you listen – a partnership in listening; it is this partnership that makes rehearsals successful and engaging, that all are listening and responding.

Directing a choir is not about one person, it is about an agreed partnership where one person is guiding the whole to being better, but it is a partnership. That one person directing is in service to that partnership and this should always be the attitude toward the relationship.

Should a conductor be in the unfortunate position of not being prepared it will be obvious to all. I have sat in a rehearsal room and watched an ill-prepared conductor work in minute detail on a piece of music simply because they heard one element that was not correct; on working on this one detail for a woefully long period, the choir began firing questions at them out of the sheer frustration of not being able to rehearse all the other bars of music and feel the achievement of having completed a movement, a section or the whole work ; this frustration causes the choir to lack in confidence in the partnership between them and their conductor and the singing became less engaged and less musical as a result. The rehearsal was not a comfortable experience for either the choir or the conductor as a result.

I do not think it wise to assume the choir is not self-aware. Rather, I think it best to assume that they are fully aware of what may not be working or what is working. That is not to say that they are always listening but that they are usually 'aware'.

The consequences of not listening whilst directing

Not listening properly and objectively (by objectively I mean keeping ourselves grounded, present in the room and not 'away in an imagined artistic and emotional mindscape) to the vocal ensemble we are directing will mean that:

- We suggest to the singers we are leading that we do not care about how they sound or what performance standard the upcoming public sharing will advertise
- We will miss the inaccuracies that could easily be corrected with rehearsal
- We may end up with an uneven vocal tone (unblended)
- Individual voices may suddenly become stronger in performance as they have not been tempered in rehearsal
- Diction, clarity, and all text work may be variable and with limited success
- There may be a general lack of confidence in an upcoming performance which will breed negativity
- General ensemble discipline will be unaddressed and so the choir will sound under prepared, even to the casual listener

We are all human. The examples of what stop singers from listening equally apply to those who direct or lead vocal groups. In chapter 2 the examples I gave were:
1. Personal thoughts and concerns from our personal life or receiving an unasked-for personal remark that is upsetting
2. Your opinion on the music being sung
3. Not having prepared and so not knowing the music
4. General disinterest because of an internal issue with the choir or its management
5. Eating and drinking - a lack or need
6. Illness
7. Disagreement with an individual related to the choir over music interpretation or language skills or some other technical facet of direction

I am sure there are other reasons we could put into categories but perhaps for conductors the one skill we need is to be prepared for any of the above to occur, and, to be able to find ways of managing incidents like those mentioned in a way that does not detract or distract from our listening and allows us to fulfil the role of directing our singers.

How Conductors can Tell that Members of their Choir Stopped Listening

The number of subliminal messages communicated between a choir and its leader — and vice versa — is quite remarkable. What is also remarkable is how many of those subliminal messages are consciously registered by members of the choir or the conductor. A good choral conductor will be able to read the faces and small actions of the choir members, sensing when it is time for a comfort break for example. Here are some subliminal messages and signs that conductors can receive from their choir during a rehearsal:

Lack of eye contact. Looking away, staring into space, observing other members, glancing at the floor, not focusing on the score. The position of the eyes is clear and obvious to interpret by the person standing at the front, and to those sitting near

Inappropriate posture. Slouching, crossing legs, folding arms (which means singers are not holding their score properly), leaning to one side, putting an arm around the next person — all potentially tell that a singer is not listening as fully as they should

Self-distraction. Doodling, fidgeting, yawning, checking the time, looking into a pocket mirror, itching, scratching, picking noses, adjusting clothing – all signs that someone has stopped listening

Facial Expressions. There are some members of choirs who concentrate quite hard on communicating through facial expression. They do it with those sitting close to them, those sitting on the opposite side of the room and even those leading. The expressions themselves can show everything from sublime happiness to vehement disapproval. Some people prefer to hide their feelings, while others feel entitled to show that they are very happy or unhappy about something. Sometimes leaders tolerate this but at other times they may choose not to. But regardless of the situation and feelings involved, concentrating hard on maintaining a particular facial expression — and making sure that others see this expression — means that a singer is no longer listening and that their contribution is compromised.

There are other signs of disassociations from the rehearsal. Here are some more examples.

Asking irrelevant or unrelated questions. A singer might suddenly ask a question that comes from seemingly nowhere or may relate to a different section or movement, interrupting the flow of the rehearsal

Repeating a question that has just been answered. Quite commonly, a question is asked twice. It might have been asked by a member at the front of the choir but the answer wasn't quite heard in the back. The reason for this is noise distraction by someone not listening, usually

Daydreaming. Musing or daydreaming is also common and might even be sparked by an idea or thought shared by the leader of the choir

Offering unsolicited advice. A singer, who may have attended a previous rehearsal with a different choir or conductor, may want to advise others about a movement before the conductor has the opportunity to cover the same point. The singer may do this in a bid to contribute a different or interesting thought about the passage involved. This may be a good thing, but singers should be encouraged to wait for an appropriate time, rather than interrupt the flow or pace of the rehearsal. Not waiting for an appropriate time shows that a singer is too distracted in wanting to share their useful 'nugget of information' to listen to what it is happening in the rehearsal room.

In this chapter, we have been through several reasons why conductors or singers might stop listening in a rehearsal, or how they might be stopped from listening in a rehearsal. We have also discussed some possible ways in which we show those around us that we have stopped listening.

The next chapter discusses how, in our own disciplined way, we can learn to listen in a rehearsal, why we should listen and what we should listen for.

Chapter 3: How To Listen and What To Listen For

The predominant activity conductors do is listen. Yes, they beat time, yes their gestures are designed to help recall or mirror the musical direction on the page and anything else added, yes they encourage those singers before them, yes they spend many hours poring over scores and preparing for rehearsals by making notes but none of these things are of any use if a conductor does not *listen*.

If you are a conductor who enjoys being the centre of attention whilst beating your arms for a group of singers to follow you because of your own self-belief, listening to the singers before you may not always be your priority. As a result, you may not always achieve the outcome you want or may not always hear what is happening in your rehearsals at all.

The wonderful thing about choirs is their humanity — a group of individuals who come together to rehearse with the goal of performing as a unified team of singers who enjoy making music together. Whether the choir is a community choir, an 'office 'choir, a choral society, a male voice choir, a youth choir, a female voice choir, an LGBTQ+ choir, a chamber choir, a barbershop chorus, a church choir, a symphonic chorus or a 1,000 voices strong massed choir. There is one thing they have in common: passion and belief in singing together. That togetherness can be honed to create something uniquely joyful — an ensemble event.

But it requires humility. Humility on behalf of the singers to listen to the conductor give clear and concise instructions to improve the music making — and to accept and respond to it accordingly - as well as humility on behalf of the conductor to not desire to denigrate the unique sound formed by the singers but to want to enhance its standard.

Listening is a difficult thing for conductors — a lot of the time we are required to listen whilst doing other things, such as beating time or gesturing musical direction. Listening is a skill that can and must be developed by all conductors looking for successful results. Without listening, objectively, we will find that choral success is elusive.

It is quite easy to tell if a conductor is not listening during a rehearsal. Here are some things that can occur when a leader is *not* listening:

- The rehearsal stops and starts as the conductor is aware that things are not quite right but cannot decide what it is that is wrong
- The rehearsal is moved along at a fast pace without the conductor making notes of or acknowledging the things that need work on; the choir might become aware of this and takes a step back in confidence
- Members of the choir, in frustration, ask to rehearse certain sections again because they can hear that something needs work and do not want to let the moment pass.
- Text clarity and diction suffer when the conductor does not hear the different pronunciations, diphthongs, elision, and vowel shapes. Because the conductor does not hear them, they are not made uniform and remain unclear.
- Some sections of the music being rehearsed end up not being looked at in greater detail and are still the same by the time of the performance. The result is a performance with blemishes.
- Listening becomes easier if the conductor has adequately prepared the score for directing. Adequate preparation highlights all the sections a conductor might need to work on and fix, to attain accuracy and inspire confidence.

Ideally, conductors should know any score they will direct a rehearsal or performance of so intimately that they read the score and simultaneously hear how it sounds in their head – their own recording if you like. Comparing how it *should* sound to what it *does* sound like in the rehearsal room, makes it easier to hear discrepancies or things that can be 'fixed' and made better.

We are all used to listening in a rehearsal but sometimes it is worth reflecting on what exactly we should be listening for when working with a group of singers. At its most basic, singing in a choir is a collaborative process which needs everyone to commit to the learning and bettering of singing together. We have established that listening helps singers to:

- Understand the music being sung and the instructions needed to create it to the best possible standard
- Help our enjoyment (of a rehearsal and/or performance)
- Collect information on the music we are singing which might help understand the context in which it was written
- Enable us to learn.

A bit like being in a classroom, singers who want to learn and develop their skills should listen to those around them — as their fellow singers can give them hints and tips without even realising — as well as to those leading the rehearsal.

The Pre-Rehearsal Regime for Aiding Your Singer's Practice – Preparing Singers to Listen

The most committed singers in any choir create a pre-rehearsal regime for themselves, like players in a rugby or football team do. That pre-rehearsal regime might spread over more than one day; it could be that two or three evenings before a rehearsal session are spent looking over the music, singing whilst playing the notes on a keyboard or other instrument, listening to the music being rehearsed with a CD or downloaded recording or getting together with others in the same voice section to learn together. If a regular pre-rehearsal regime is established, it will go a long way to help anyone learn the music and therefore be ready to listen to what is occurring in the rehearsal room.

As a conductor, on the day of a rehearsal, you might find the following Do's and Don'ts useful when thinking about the rehearsal session itself:

DO:
- Remember this rehearsal is for the singers — it's 'their time'
- Ensure that everyone switches off their mobile devices at the start of the rehearsal — make it part of your regime
- Check that singers have a pencil or e-pencil to hand to mark up their score as necessary

- Encourage your singers to 'react' in the rehearsal — to listen to you and others around them and to acknowledge when they have instituted instructed changes well into their singing and started creating more nuance in their music-making.

DON'T:
- Check your own mobile device for messages or mail. Remember to focus.
- Plan your direction of a piece too concretely in advance — whilst rehearsing you may wish to implement changes if the singing is going well or the opposite
- Try to multitask in a rehearsal — one thing at a time and if you need to confirm an instruction check that your singers have all heard it properly (do not be afraid to do this, there will always be someone who wants to ask for confirmation)
- Think about outside events like eating, online or in-person meetings, work, or family. This is 'rehearsal time.'

A good choir will have ensured that the person leading is qualified to do so musically and/or has gained a lot of experience working with choirs to enable successful rehearsals and concert performances.

To sing successfully together, all choir members must accept that the conductor is going to coach them to understand the music and the various techniques needed to achieve the best choral sound. From the podium or music stand, a conductor not only conducts, keeping the choir in time with itself and with any accompanying instruments but listens carefully to the choirs' ensemble sound. The conductor then directs the choir to 'iron out any creases' and to help the choir be the best they can, as well as ensuring that the musical directions on the score are followed. Any extra 'interpretative qualities' that the conductor wants are added to the choirs' performance, including phrasing, breath marks, tempi, musical dynamics and other commands that will make the performance worthy of listening to — by an audience and by the choir itself.

How To Listen During a Rehearsal

This takes practice and discipline. It is an important discipline for all who want the best for their choir. Here are some things to consider when trying to listen during a rehearsal:

Pay Attention. Our attention can easily wander. Learn to keep as focused as possible. When directing the choir, provide them with clear explanations. Most singers want to know why they are being asked to do something. Write your direction down into your score. Do not be afraid to nod when your direction has been followed to acknowledge that it has made a difference and don't be afraid to reiterate instructions if you feel the singers have not fully understood them.

Focus. Be aware of the sound your singers are making and then focus on the sound of certain voice sections compared with others. When you are comfortable with that, focus on each vocal section, then two voice sections together and then the whole ensemble

Give feedback. If your singers have understood your instructions or you feel that something is going well, acknowledge this with the choir. Singers are, after all, human, and they will appreciate it if their execution of musical direction is noticed and appreciated, and the effect or result acknowledged as better than before. This helps build trust between conductor and singers as well as the singer's confidence — and shows that you have been listening to the response to what was being asked for.

Defer judgement. Some singers don't necessarily agree with a particular musical direction or interpretational point that is being asked for. Best practice is to acknowledge it but defer judgement. If someone flags something up, it's best to thank them for their feedback whether it's agreeable, or not. Discussing opinions on a musical matter will distract from the rehearsal and will certainly distract from listening and focus. Good choir members will note, defer and then discuss matters with the conductor privately or if their voice section has a 'voice section representative', they will raise it with them for discussion with you at a discrete opportunity. We should be prepared however, to manage the sometimes-difficult scenario where a singer raises an objection publicly in the rehearsal. In short, opinions might stop the choir from listening at a crucial point, so try to deal with them positively, effectively and quickly.

Appropriate responses. Your rehearsals are a period where you may wish to 'try things out' — you may want to add in different interpretations of the music, including changes to the dynamics, tempi, phrasing or even adding cuts to the music. A singer's response to instruction should always be appropriate. Appropriate responses are smiling, nodding, writing things down and then immediately attempting to do what is being asked for. Inappropriate responses may be involuntary or not. These can include tutting, shaking the head, sitting back in the chair and slumping, not writing things down, looking anywhere but at the person speaking. A good member of a choir will listen attentively and avoid inappropriate responses and adverse effects on the choir. A wise leader will intuitively decide whether to call out negative behaviour during a rehearsal or to maintain focus but address it later, privately.

Preparing to Listen – 'pre-match regime' for Conductors

Committed conductors should have a regime that builds towards the first rehearsal of any music. In essence, conductors need to be prepared.

Preparation should consist of:

- Following a score of the music chosen whilst listening to a recording
- Reading the score and understanding the text of what is being sung
- Analysing the score to understand the musical structure and the compositional intent (which in turn aids and informs gestural nuance and interpretation)
- Researching or reading around the history and development of the music so that its compositional context is understood

- Learning the vocal parts for each voice section to be able to recall them and compare them to the learning in the rehearsal room
- Learning the score: conducting it (without a reference recording) to the point where one can 'hear' the music internally and conduct one's way through the score in front of a mirror, being able to cue vocal entries, conduct and gesture the tempi, dynamics, phrasing and breath as necessary
- If a full score includes orchestration, be able to navigate the score and learn the instrumental entries and their relationship to the choral entries so that one can successfully cue these and know where they are, when they are and why they are
- When analysing the vocal parts, highlight any passages that are demanding or may present vocal difficulties (examples are large or chromatic intervals, unusual or challenging voice leading or harmony, or vowels that are in the extremes of the vocal ranges)
- Decide on the consonant placements at the end of phrases
- Mark any additional vocal effects or dynamics that could be added to the published directions to enhance the performance

How to listen during a rehearsal

Listening skills during a rehearsal take time and practice to develop. Conductors must be able to hear the good the bad and the indifferent; by that I mean: **M.A.I.I.V.E.**
An acronym for:
    MUSICALITY
    ACCURACY
    INTERPRETATION
    INTONATION
    VOICES
    ENSEMBLE

    All the practical elements that make up **M.A.I.I.V.E.** can be listened for separately whilst rehearsing. These are general elements that contribute to music making by vocal ensembles and it would be wise to develop the skill of listening whilst focussing on one of these elements at a time before developing the listening so that it encompasses more than one of these elements simultaneously. Choose one or two elements to help focus your listening and then widen your listening by choosing more elements to add. If you listen 'under these headlines' you will find that your own listening will become more objective, accurate, analytical and effective.

Good conductors will have prepared their scores for listening to whilst directing a live rehearsal, under these headlines, whether using a commercial recording or just the score itself enough to be adequately prepared to guide the choir through its preparation to performance.

Listening Practice Away from the Rehearsal Room

Investing in time and practice to listen can pay great dividends in and away from the rehearsal room. It is worth developing a listening regime with your singers, particularly when it comes to music and music-making. Here are some ways of practising listening skills when away from the rehearsal room, you might like to suggest to your ensemble:

Learning Aids. With today's technology, it is possible that some of the music you are currently rehearsing is available online. Learning aids might include an electronic or human-voice recording of a particular voice part. New 'apps' are developed all the time to help conductors prepare individual learning aids. Start by doing an online search for learning aids for the musical items you need to learn. If not, approach your choir to see if they might fund a way to create them (but always bear in mind music copyright laws). Use these learning aids to support your choir in getting to know their voice parts. Ask the singers to rehearse with the aids at home as often as they are able. You will be surprised at how quickly your singers develop confidence as their recall and accuracy develop through the rehearsal period.

Creating homemade sectional recordings or learning aids. If you are so inspired, supporting your choir by creating homemade recordings of the vocal line for each voice section will always be appreciated. The only thing to bear in mind are the music copyright laws in relation to the work(s) you are learning. Seek advice on this and don't make recordings to distribute until the necessary checks have been undertaken and permissions sought and granted.

Listen to commercial recordings. Most of us own a CD player or home system, tablet, or mobile device to access music-streaming platforms or apps. There is every likelihood that a recording of the musical item you are rehearsing is available for purchase or download. Listening to others perform the current repertoire you are rehearsing is an excellent opportunity for you and your group to listen to the 'entire landscape' of the piece, all the voices and any accompaniment. Here are some of the advantages of seeking out a recording:

- You can listen to the whole work
- You can listen to pick out a voice section
- If you listen closely, you may hear extraneous noises from the recording room or even the occasional musical error.

The point is that everyone's general familiarity with the work will improve and the understanding gained from listening to the recording will help bolster confidence in the rendition of the piece. This, in turn, will make it easier to listen to what is happening during a rehearsal or performance.

Get-Togethers. Singing in a choir should be a fun but demanding hobby that your singers enjoy. So why not ask them to schedule a 'voice-section get-together' away from the rehearsal room, for a group of like-minded singers to get together and learn or rehearse the vocal lines in a less formal setting, say at someone's home? A good choir will always socialise together in one way or another – a choir who bond well together are relaxed enough to sing and listen together and make a much better blended choral sound. More on blending voices in chapters 4 and 9.

Next, I have set out a small excerpt of music. Spend some time looking only at the music. If you can read music, try singing your vocal line or any of the others. Then work out what you might expect to listen out for whilst rehearsing it. If you do not read music, this example should not stop you from doing the same thing. See if you can follow more than one line simultaneously, whether it moves up and down in pitch, whether it is rhythmic or not, and where you might be able to breathe. Following the music, I will then list some of the things that we can glean from the excerpt by listening. Let's compare notes!

Breathing. All voices should breathe on the commas in the text. Altos and tenors (bar 5, beat 2 altos, beat 3 tenors) should be careful not to cut the quaver short before the comma; there is more space there to breathe on the comma than looks on the page!

Tempo. The score is marked as '*Lento*', which translates as 'slow', but the crotchet marking next to it, is 60 crotchets per minute. That's one beat a second, so don't allow the music to drag by holding onto your breath. Instead, sing through each phrase and use your breath to do so — breathe it in and sing it out. Follow where the conductor places the beats and pace your breath accordingly – and keep listening to the whole choir, so that you are singing at tempo and evenly together.

Dynamics. There are specific markings here for all voice parts. Let's take some time to become aware of the *piano* or 'quiet' marking at the beginning of the Alto and Bass lines, to ensure that one voice part is not louder than the other on those opening notes. Altos and Basses should also note that their opening dynamic is *p cresc* or *piano crescendo*. The choir will rehearse that growth of dynamic together and listen to one another as the sound develops. Being able to hear each section is essential, there is no need to 'over-sing'.

Rhythm. Singers should be careful to observe the tied notes — it helps to push some extra air through the system on a tie. Ask them to listen to the added vocal colour (quality) it brings when they do this. Each section member should listen carefully to the others when they sing through a tie — they can be danger spots for individual voices to sing a little too loudly and so can be heard, which can distract from the overall choral sound. Altos and Tenors need to be careful not to accentuate the semiquaver motif in bar 5 and to keep it as smooth or *legato* as possible.

Equalise voice parts. Given that only two voice parts begin the singing in bar 1, it is important that the choir listens to itself and the sound it is creating to ensure that each of the four voice parts sounds equal. If the Sopranos and Tenors (the upper voices) don't listen to the dynamics and volume being created by the Altos and Basses (the lower voice), they cannot 'match' the dynamics already 'set up'. There is then potential for the upper voices to start singing on a radically different dynamic to the lower voices. As a result, the whole piece will sound out of balance and 'uneven'.

Diction. Altos and Basses will benefit from practising the 'k' sound at the beginning of the word 'kyrie' for their entry to sound together. It's a hard consonant sound with no pitch – a consonant plosive. But rather than shying away from what might be a loud consonant sound, make sure to articulate it together, on the beat. We'll practice this by watching the conducted beat, breathing together and then sounding the 'k' so the outbreath for the hard 'k' sound is on the beat. Listen to your section as we do this and when you're feeling confident, start listening to the other sections too. 'Cross-sectional listening' is a must to keep everyone together for that opening entry. Tenors and Sopranos must also not shy away from sounding their 'k's' – in some ways even more so because they do not start singing at bar 1. The choir and the audience all want to hear their entries when they happen, so don't try to 'dampen' the 'k' sound, let it ring. A note for all of us — the vowel sounds after the 'k' are the ones to keep at the dynamic on the page, we can control the dynamics in vowels much easier! The choir sings the word 'kyrie' a lot; to create a 'forward sounding 'ee' for 'kee-ree-eh', shape the lips a bit like a kiss. Don't sing a 'flat' 'ee' vowel with the mouth shaped liked a toothy grin — the sound created that way is uncontrollable and too overbearing; also, the epiglottic funnel (see chapter 11) will be squeezed closed in a way which mean the singer may have to force more air through the vocal cords and out, causing unnecessary vocal tension. Instead, try a subtle 'ee' with lips forward. Listen to yourself as you practice this vowel at home.

Listening — Rehearsal Room or Home

We can encourage singers to answer these questions internally as they listen to themselves singing with others or with a recording or a learning aid:

- Do I sound louder, quieter or the same as everyone else?
- Do I breathe in the same places as everyone else?
- Am I running out of breath anywhere? If so, do I know why? If I don't, I should seek advice from a singing teacher or a conductor
- Am I making the right 'ee' shape as the conductor mentioned above?
- Can I hear an individual's voice within the section?
- Am I phrasing the words in the same way as my section? If not, why not?
- Have I got all the notes right?
- Am I singing a different rhythm to others in any places? If I am, I need to ask for clarification on what is correct
- Am I trying to keep my consonants quiet? If so, why?
- Am I singing 'in tune'? If not, what could be the cause? If I'm not sure, I should ask someone
- Am I pronouncing the words correctly/the same as others in my section?

Above everything else, this list requires you to be used to actively listening as a singer. Listening to yourself can be difficult and off-putting; nevertheless, conductors should encourage all singers in a choir to do so. Many of us have winced when we've heard our own speaking voices recorded and played back to us because we are not often aware how different we sound to others from how we sound in our own heads and bodies. Singing in a choir will inevitably start to magnify the sound of a singer's voice to themselves but if when they sing your members learn to listen to themselves in context with others, a breakthrough may occur in relation to the general blend of sound by a choir.

When we coach singers into accepting how their voices sound - their limitations and quirks – we make an important step forward in everyone's listening habits.

Chapter 4: Listening for ensemble

What is ensemble?

The dictionary term for the word ensemble is "...a group of musicians, actors or dancers who regularly perform together." Also, "An ensemble of things or people is a group of things or people considered as a whole rather than as separate individuals." - *Collins English Dictionary*.

In the choral sense, when we talk about ensemble, we are discussing the act of making music together, with our voices, as a whole and not as individuals. The act and art of ensemble can be developed and curated by a conductor who is familiar with all the elements that contribute to ensemble singing. It is worth describing them in this context (as elements) as these are also the common elements that can be worked on if they are not accurate or musical within the ensemble singing. These elements cannot be ascertained without listening:

Breathing

A successful choir is aware of its breathing, the noise it makes when it breathes in and out, the need for correct breathing in order to secure solid opening entries and well supported phrases, the need for breath to be treated as an important relation to the music itself: many choir members forget that the breath they are using is for a purpose – to help create different effects or 'colours', if you like, in the voice, which enable both musical notes and text to take on meaning and interpretation, as well as having an emotional content. Breathing also supports the shaping and execution of consonant and vowel sounds and the way that a singer uses and engages with their breath – the *intent* of the breath – is not something that is coached by all choral conductors. Breathing is not just a means to singing, it can open a real vista of different vocal techniques, effects, tones and timbres but all of this is connected to breathing.

The intent behind a breath

It is easy to relax into singing in a choral rehearsal if the music is familiar. If the music is less than familiar the singers are still 'learning' the vocal line. Once the learning period is over and the true rehearsal period begins (and I'm including all amateur and professional choirs here) then the true coaching of how to sing phrases, how to introduce a vocal colour palette* (and what that palette* consists of for the piece in hand) and the coaching of breath control and breath use against the framework of the music in hand, begins. It is advantageous to coach singers in the use of their breath; all too often choral singers simply breath in to inhale and breath out to exhale, without thinking of how to use to the breath they have inhaled to help sustain a consistent tone during exhalation. Sometimes choral singers simply allow their breath to carry them through until they feel the need to breathe in again and this can form a habitual pattern over a set number of beats and notes. However, the use of breathing exercises as part of a warm up should always be connected to the coaching of breath control through certain phrases when rehearsing a work; choral singers often have a greater lung capacity than they would give themselves credit for; as conductors we need to have mapped out the breathing patterns and then be listening to ensure that the ensemble is kept intact by everyone using the same breathing, the same inhalation with the intention of singing through a phrase or phrases, using this breath in a constructive way, with good abdominal and diaphragmatic support to aid its use. Some members will shy away from 'breaking out' of their own 'established need' to breathe after 2 bars in 4/4 time but with coaching and encouragement, many choral singers can improve both the longevity and use of their breath to really connect to their music making, helping to make their contribution even more personal and, as a result, energising and humane.

First syllable entries

The first time a choir opens its mouth to sing – the very first phrase of music it sings together – is critical. Then the beginning of every phrase that follows is as critical. The opening sound and shape and formation of the first text, the first consonant, vowel and syllable are important.

Why? Because in the moment it takes to form a choral entry, a choir can communicate its effectiveness, its sense of ensemble, its discipline, and its unity. In other words, it gives its level of musicianship away, to anyone listening. Therefore, that first beat of a choir singing is important because it shows immediately whether this is a listening choir, or not.

Phrasing

Coaching your singers to align the use of their breath with the framework of the text helps to ensure a good relationship between singing the words, their expression brings the meaning of the text to life and accurately depicts the composers' intentions. It also helps your singers to be controlled and focussed on the delivery of the underlay – at all tempi -which is vital to an audiences' understanding and appreciation of the musical skills displayed, the compositional craft depicted and the intelligent interpretation of what is on the printed page. Phrasing of vocal music is delicate and can change the understanding of the meaning of a phrase to the listener. In the same way that we use punctuation and articulation to deliver meaning and logic to our speaking and writing of text, so we must ensure that our musical phrasing does likewise. Have all singers grasped the relationship between the text being sung and its clear communication to the listening audience?

Dynamics

As discussed in a previous chapter, every choir is unique, and every choir should be able to set its own interpretation of vocal dynamics. One choirs' *piano* might be another choirs' *pianissimo*, but each choir should be able to identify and recall its own dynamic scale. This is only achieved by the choir listening to itself, establishing its core blend sound, and working out how it sounds through each dynamic level. Exercises previously mentioned can be used to ascertain the dynamic levels and these can be fun. All choirs would benefit from agreeing the dynamic volumes, being able to recall them during rehearsals, as this makes for a more efficient and beneficial strategy for being 'performance ready'. It also stops choirs from 'over singing' dynamics and 'singing themselves into a corner' when their *forte* is actually *fortissimo*! It might sound clinical but the choir who listens, blends, and understands the relationship between each of the dynamics, is a choir on the right path to good ensemble singing.

I have found an excellent way to help choirs understand the way their ensemble dynamics sound and how the sound they produce is related to the way the dynamics are achieved:

Ask the choir (if you are a director) to hold a piece of paper directly in front of their face, no more than an inch away from the end of their nose. Now ask them to sing a well-known musical phrase from a nursery rhyme, a song, or some current repertoire. When they do this, the sound they produce will reverberate from the enclosed environment created by the paper being so close to their faces. Singers should listen to how this sounds and concentrate on singing quietly: if a whole choir does this, and then keeps the volume the same but takes away the paper, the whole choir should be singing at a *pianissimo* volume. The paper can be replaced in front of the face but now at 3 to 4 inches away from the tip of the nose; the exercise should be repeated. This time when the paper is removed and the choir sings at the same dynamic, the overall sound created should be around the *piano* level. The exercise can be repeated with the paper moving further away and thus the dynamic increasing, using the paper as a focal point for singing to. If the choir really listens to these dynamics carefully, learns to recognise what they sound like and then reproduces them within their music making, their relationship with dynamics will become much more personal as an ensemble. This 'ownership' of dynamics - as an ensemble - will help train their ears to be listening out for how the dynamics are changing as they rehearse and perform. The sense of achievement that an ensemble feels when they conquer their 'ownership' of dynamics, is always palpable and brings with it a renewed sense of confidence in the ensemble's identity.

It's core.

Intonation

In short, we use the word intonation to describe accuracy of pitch when we sing. It is not always easy, if you are singing in a choir, to hear either your own intonation or that of others, as you sit collectively in voice sections, particularly if the blend of the voice section is not settled and individual voices (often loud) are heard. An important aspect of this is to ask singers to make sure that they are using omni-directional listening. That they are listening to themselves – in context with listening to the voice section – in context with listening to the whole choir. I often ask singers to target other sections to listen to, or to listen to those sitting behind or in front (more difficult). 'Zoning' the listening in this way is a good start on the road to blending, as well as intonation.

The fascinating thing about intonation in a choir though, is that an individual's intonation is directly influenced by those around him/her/them. Therefore, it is perfectly possible for whole voice sections to have a different sense of intonation to the others, particularly if the 'sectional listening' (listening, as a section, to the whole of the choir) is under par. Fixing intonation is best done by splitting sections up from one another and replacing them afterward; it is also achieved by physical blending.

Blend

You will (I hope) read the chapter on blending. The whole sound of any choir is unique to the point that some listeners can identify which choir is singing (on a recording, say) just by listening to them. The identity, spirit, soul, and 'brand' of a choir lies in its own ability to create the sound it identifies itself by – like a rallying call or tribal identification. It is important that a conductor does not try to change this but rather add to it, using exercises such as are mentioned in this book. The singers in a choir get to know one another, and many become either surrogate or extended family members to each other. The blend of the choir, it's *uniquely identifying whole sound*, is as important as the music it sings. The job of a singer is to contribute to this whole sound by allowing their voices to become immersed in it, without losing touch with their own individual sound – something that can be coached with the right exercises and diplomacy – and the job of a conductor is to encourage this whole sound, 'iron out the creases' and to help develop and curate it. As mentioned previously, choirs with non-blending voices are just a group of individual voices who happen to be singing together. It is important then that both intonation and blending are addressed in every rehearsal, directly or in-directly through coaching.

Diction and elision

The way a choir interprets text can be hugely contributory to its reputation. No audience member wishes to sit in a public performance trying to work out what the choir is singing about.

As mentioned previously, the discipline of well placed, crisp but not elongated consonants, well-shaped 'Italianate' vowels and the way a choir deals with diphthongs and sounds that could be elided if not sung with accompanying small diphthongs or vowels, is an important one. It pays dividends; if the choir has successfully worked on its enunciation, the text will carry forward clearly to an audience in any performance and any performance acoustic. Even in cathedrals with seconds of delay to the sound carrying around the nave!

We cannot hope to aid our choirs with direction for good diction without listening to them and correcting through the rehearsal process, with positive coaching.

Vowels and consonants

The sounds that make up words. Each word can be carefully created with breath support, intent of breath, crisp clean consonants (voiced or unvoiced), diphthongs where necessary to create those tricky textual colours we are so used to in speech without dispensing with musicality and taking care of lazy or natural elision.

Rhythm

Creating correct rhythm together is a tricky skill, particularly if the rhythm is either not on strong beats or involves smaller notes like semi-quavers. Difficult but by no means impossible. Listening to the choir create the correct rhythms together in a piece of music that is not 'straight forward crotchets and minims' can be a real joy to both singer and conductor. The root of this, as previously mentioned, is good ensemble work. The willingness to commit as an individual, a row of singers and friends, a voice section, or a whole choir, to learning the correct rhythm and learning the accompanying vocal techniques to allow that rhythm to carry – together - is vital. Also vital is not giving up! Exercises surrounding the learning of rhythmic passages - or sometimes just a dotted crotchet followed by a quaver - should involve basic 'listen and repeat' routines; there is no simpler way than to listen and then try to repeat the rhythm you have heard. The question is whether you simultaneously learn pitch and rhythm or whether you separate them out first and then sing them together. My advice is to always keep it simultaneous, for efficiency's sake.

Posture

Singing is a craft that can be developed and refined. It is one of the most personal things we can do as an expressive art. Singing well is something we all want to attain, and singers certainly don't want to let the others in their voice section down by not being prepared enough.

Rehearsals themselves can be demanding as well as fun. After about an hour of intense engagement in a rehearsal our bodies naturally try to tell us that it might be nice to relax for a period. We can find ourselves relaxing into the back of our chairs, our shoulders and heads may sag, our music copies end up in our laps, we yawn we stretch…. we stop listening.

Posture plays a huge part in being able to sing properly – our vocal and support mechanisms (all the biological bits we use to sing with) need the proper shape and space to work properly. If our bodies over-relax our pitching and intonation, vowel and consonant creation, diction and blend can all be affected. A good conductor will remind singers of the need for the right posture if they see the choir beginning to sag! Here are some pointers for good singing posture:

- Feet shoulder length apart
- Legs straight but not rigid
- Upper body slightly elevated from the abdomen (test this by stretching up then bringing your arms to your side whilst keeping your upper body in the same position as you were stretching)
- Head looking directly forward, chin in neutral position (neither up nor down)
- Chest should not be stuck outwards too much but there should be a feeling that the rib cage is trying to 'hang over' the abdomen
- Music copies should be held so that we can read them and see the conductor just over the top of the page

If you direct a choir and have struggled with the general ensemble, I hope that some of the above will be of help so that the choir you work with can develop, one element at a time, toward the goal of excellent ensemble singing. Listen as each of these elements change the way the choir sounds.

For vocal colour palette, read set dynamics, phrasing, vocal tone and timbre, breath control and articulation of rhythm, accents, and text

Chapter 5: Active listening, Exercises, Vowels and Consonants

Whether you are a singer, a conductor or both, there is one fact about listening that is worth noting: if it can, it will get in the way or be forgotten. Listening is the one discipline that is most easily dispensed with, whether you sing or conduct a community choir, a rock choir, a chamber choir, or a symphonic chorus.

The more a choir listens to itself, the more attuned it becomes. It will recognise when the music is sounding good and when the music needs work. We cannot make music together unless we listen to its process — together.

This chapter outlines several exercises designed to help singers - during workshops or rehearsals - regain the discipline of listening whilst working on repertoire. You can use these exercises during any part of the rehearsal where listening needs underlining. Singers may want to do these exercises at home on their own, with a friend or in small groups — away from the rehearsal room, in preparation for the next session.

Why Should we Listen to Ourselves?

Most of the following exercises require a device that allows you to record yourself on — a dictation machine or a mobile phone is ideal. Most mobile devices and electronic tablets have a 'memo recording app' on them these days, so find where it is on your device and get ready to use it:

Six Exercises for Breath, Notes, Phrasing, Pitching, Timekeeping

Exercise 1: First breath
With either a piece of music in mind or a vocal score/copy of the music in front of you, select a section of music you know well (this works equally well with 'popular' music as it does with 'classical' music) and sing through it. It does not have to be very long, a couple of

phrases perhaps, but sing through it in your head only, making no external noise at all. Do this a couple of times. When you have done so, either listen closely or record yourself singing the same portion of music out loud. Did you hear the amount of sound you created when breathing in to prepare to sing? If you didn't, sing it again and have a closer listen! Now, imagine if all the people you sing with made the same noise at the same time… it would be quite a loud intake of breath! Go back to singing the portion of music you chose in your head again. After a couple of go's, sing it out loud again but this time control your intake of breath over a longer period before you begin to sing — control its intake and therefore the sound you make as you breathe in. Rehearse yourself into controlling your intake (which will become deeper over time) for all your prepared breaths — especially at the beginning of a piece of music or a new section. You are now listening to how you start singing — even before you sing! This is the first step towards listening to yourself and being comfortable with it.

Exercise 2: First notes

How our voices sound when we begin new musical phrases, or whole pieces of music is important. Should our voices sound like they are faltering, it can (unknowingly) have an impact on our confidence or even the confidence of singers around us, whether during a rehearsal or performance. Therefore, we should take a collective responsibility to build up confidence in our breathing and then in the way we use our breath as we begin to sing.

Again, select a passage of music that you are working on and sing it through in your head. After that, prepare your breath and sing only the first syllable or word. Repeat this as many times as it takes for you to feel prepared to sing that first musical note and word or syllable wholly and confidently. When you feel happy about this, either listen closely or record yourself singing. How does it sound? Here are some questions to ask yourself:

- Did I prepare my breath well?
- Did I sound the consonant letters of the syllable or word without trying to dampen them/soften them/over-sing them?
- How did the vowels sound?

Note that 'well-placed' vowels will be in tune and that vowels that need some work may affect tuning, which is where a recording device really is useful. Do not worry about things sounding somewhat 'out of tune' or 'flat' — repeat the exercise noting which vowels could do with being sung with a more open mouth or the bottom jaw lowered more and try out different mouth positions. Re-record or listen to yourself closely. As you isolate these things they will improve and you will become accustomed to making the right shapes with your mouth to ensure that your personal tuning remains consistent; this will, in turn, feed into your personal confidence as a singer. Being able to listen to yourself whilst learning how your mouth makes the correct shapes and contours to ensure your singing voice is consistent of tone and manages all the different sounds that text can make, is an important part of becoming comfortable with it. It sounds obvious but when you are personally comfortable and understanding of your own mouth and annunciation through it, you will be able to respond quicker and more effectively if, as a musical director, you ask for a specific sound for a particular word or passage. The more you do this the more you will become aware when singers are not quite getting it right.

Exercise 3: Phrasing

Once you feel comfortable that your breath is well prepared and that the first word or syllable sounds clear, it is time to extend the exercise to a complete musical phrase or passage. The one addition to note here is the use of that prepared breath. You should now try to use all the breath you have taken in to sing through each phrase or section, until you reach some punctuation in the text or a note or bar where you as musical director might specifically suggest a breathing point. Remember to check for solid sounding of the consonants and good placement of the vowels so that the singing remains in tune; remember to either listen closely or record the choir singing through phrase after phrase, acknowledging where there may be some faults to fix. Decide on what the faults are (some examples below), isolate them and work on them to fix them, then rehearse the phrases and sections again with the 'fixes' in place:

- Are the consonants sounded clearly?
- Are the vowels shaped correctly?

- Am I preparing my breaths well, even in between phrases?
- Am I keeping to a steady tempo?
- Did I cut short any notes or words to 'fit in' a breath? If so, can I change that to make it work?
- Should I be rehearsing the dynamics now too?

By taking all these things into account when you are alone, you are advancing your knowledge and understanding of the music you are preparing, or at the very least, you may be ready to respond to pertinent questions asked during rehearsals, so that others can benefit from knowing the answers. Your listening is becoming more sensitive and adept.

Exercise 4: Testing your pitching – octaves

This exercise requires you to hum the same note at a medium, high, and low pitch. If you are unsure about how to sing octaves, imagine singing a scale – doh-re-mi-fa-soh-lah-ti-doh. An octave is the first 'doh' and the second 'doh' — notes 1 and 8 of a scale. Now record yourself humming the first 'doh' or note 1 of a scale. Do so for quite a long time. If you run out of breath, just breathe and continue. Then play the recording of you humming back to yourself. Whilst listening to the recording, hum the top 'doh' or note 8 of the scale; they should sound the same except the version on the recording is a lower one. As you hum the upper one along with yourself, listen to yourself humming live, then listen to yourself humming on the recording, all whilst keeping the humming going. Do they sound like the same note? Does your live (or recorded) note waiver? This 'pitch matching' exercise is a good way to start listening to yourself. As you listen to your recorded self, close your eyes, and make your live humming be as close as possible to the volume on the recording. It's your own voice twice over, after all! This exercise is also a great introduction to another type of choral discipline — voice blending. More on this later.

Exercise 5: Testing your pitching — scales

Singers should be familiar with singing scales – eight notes, starting at any comfortable pitch. Using Doh-Re-Mi-Fa-Soh-Lah-Ti-Doh is a good way to remember that all the notes move up one step at a time. If you are unsure about this, seek out someone who will know and ask them to record a scale for you.

Record yourself singing a scale and play it back to see how it sounds. Does it all sound in tune? If you are unsure, record yourself singing along to a recorded scale from an instrument or someone else singing. Compare each note you sing with what is sounding on the recorded version. Practise until you can sing a scale well. When you are comfortable with this, practise the scale but this time sing every other note in your head.

When you can do this fluidly, record yourself singing the scale with 'missing' notes. When you play it back, only sing the missing notes so between your recorded self and your 'live' self, you complete the scale. If possible, record yourself or listen closely to the results of the 'recorded you' and 'live you' singing together. Are the notes consistent and in tune? If not, work on it until the vocals sound seamless between the recorded and live interactions. This exercise is a simple one but does focus your listening to 'fill in' missing notes; you are training yourself to listen whilst singing in this exercise – a skill we all need whether we sing in or lead a choir.

Exercise 6: Rounds

A 'round' is a simple tune designed to be repeatable over itself even before it has come to an end. Some famous rounds that spring to mind are 'Frere Jacques' and 'London's Burning'. You will need to learn a round for this exercise.

When you have memorised your 'round', record yourself singing it. Then play it back to yourself and experiment with singing alongside it but at a different time than the recording. An easy version is starting to sing after the first phrase — so after 'Frere Jacques, Frere Jacques…' or 'London's Burning, London's Burning…'. When you can do this successfully and keep in total time and dynamic with your recording, find other more difficult entry points to start singing from. Purposely make it more difficult for yourself each time — perhaps try singing 'off-beat' or just a beat behind the recording. To make the round work at any entry point, you must concentrate on singing your own line whilst listening to the recorded line – and this multi-tasking whilst singing is a great discipline to develop.

Vowels

The shape that our mouths create when singing influence two important parts of the singing voice: it can affect the flow of breath in and out and it can affect the tuning of pitch. With that in mind, the following exercises are designed to help singers find the correct mouth shapes for certain vowels. Everyone has a different mouth that can create different shapes; these exercises are designed to be 'one size fits all'. The five primary vowels are:

AAH – As in m*ar*ket

EH – as in v*et*

EE – as in str*ee*t

OH – as in c*o*ne

OO – as in f*oo*d

Correct Shape for — Hard Palate, Soft Palate, Teeth and Tongue

AAH. Good open vowels are shaped with plenty of space toward the back of the throat and with the roof of the mouth (hard palate) raised higher than when we speak. So, the correct shape for a vowel can feel foreign to us (we can be quite lazy in our day-to-day speaking, not necessarily using a lot of our mouth). With your thumb and two fingers, make a pretend schoolyard gun shape then pop your two fingers between your teeth and bite on them gently. As you hold your fingers there, notice how wide the space feels toward the back of your mouth, your tongue has dropped to sit behind your lower teeth and the cold breeze you feel at the back of your throat indicates that your soft palate has risen. Now take your fingers out but keep your mouth in the same position. Sing an 'Aah'. It may feel 'over-opened' to you, but this is a good starting point for the long 'Aah' vowel. Experiment with this open position by putting your fingers back and then forming all the vowels (aah, eh, ee, o, ooh) whilst your fingers remain. It is possible to form all the vowels in this position. Your airway is unrestricted and so your breath flow has a clear path (it's not blocked by your soft palate at the back, the hard palate or your tongue and teeth). Try singing some passages of music you are currently working on with your choir, with your fingers in place. Then remove your fingers and try your best to keep the same shape in your mouth as you sing without them there.

EH. Think of the word 'vet' as mentioned above. Try singing it without any thought or pre-planning. Record this version if you can. Then, with your tongue in a lowered position, try singing just 'EH', then add the word 'vet'. Set your lips in the start of a smile. Record this. Compare the two recordings and note how different the 'EH' sounds are just with the lips changing position. Your lips are important when creating vowels and all words. When singing, the lips alone can influence the tuning and timbre of your vocal tone (sound of your singing).

EE. Sing only the vowel first, keep your tongue in a lowered position and sing this vowel with a slight smile. Raising your cheeks also helps your lips move into the right position.

OH. I always refer to this vowel as 'nicely rounded'. To check that the front of your mouth is in the right position, make the shape of the vowel with your lips (as in the word 'bond') and put your pointing finger in your mouth (not too far, obviously) – your finger should not brush against your lips if your 'OH' shape is rounded and big enough. Then rehearse words with this vowel, cone for example. Listen to how the slightest change in lip shape or too much relaxation in the back of your mouth can change the tuning or sound you make.

OO. The correct shape for this vowel is to pucker up as if for a kiss, then open the mouth a little further whilst slightly extending the lips again. Try singing a few words that rhyme with 'food' and experiment by changing your lip shape or the amount of space between your lips. As you listen, you will hear how easily breath flow can be interrupted.

Vowels can be easily over-sung by the mouth exaggerating the shapes needed to create them. Vowels don't need to be over-spread in the mouth. A good method for checking if singers' vowels are being placed well, is to sing through the vowel shapes whilst placing one finger from each hand on the corners of the mouth. This ensures that the mouth shapes don't get exaggerated and shows that aligned vowels are achievable by everyone, helping with the choir's overall blend.

Consonants

Words are made up of vowels and consonants. Having discussed vowels, we can see that the correct shaping of the mouth, lips, teeth, and palates play a large part in keeping our breath flow consistent, our singing in tune and our voices nicely consistent of tone. But what about consonants?

There are two different types of consonants. Voiced consonants and unvoiced consonants. The voiced consonants are B, D, G, J, L, M, N, V, W, Z. The unvoiced consonants are C, T, S. Voiced consonants can be pitched so are singable with a note. Unvoiced consonants are exactly that — a percussive, plosive sound that cannot be sung with a pitched note. It's important to note the differences between the two as we treat them differently when we sing.

Unvoiced Consonants

These consonants are almost always percussive sounds and have been designed to carry that percussive sound, so we can identify the formulation of the word around it as easily as possible.

As you practice these (choose words such as 'kyrie', 'captain', 'requiem', 'deep'), you will notice that a) hard consonants at the beginning of a word need abdominal muscle support to have the right amount of air behind them for the sound to be projected and b) hard consonants at the ends of words also need rounding off correctly so that they carry well. Ts and Ss become 'T-UH' and 'S-UH' with that small diphthong almost being just the sound of breath after it. Unvoiced consonants are there to make sounds that we should not shy away from or try to dampen, particularly if we are singing at a quieter dynamic such as *'piano'*. They must be allowed to sound. Neither should we 'hold on' to them; we should sound them well but crisply and then get past them! The inclusion of 'UH' diphthongs – that help us create a more rounded consonant (sheep-uh, corners-uh, branded-uh) help us avoid the elision of sounds even in the middle of words (more on elision later in this chapter).

Voiced Consonants

Practising singing voiced consonants in this first exercise requires us to examine the ends of a few words. We are going to sing a few words on any one note of your choosing. Choose a note that you consider to be in the medium range of your singing. We'll use the words: jumper, chair, cloth, clothed, voiced. Try singing those on one note and have a listen to how they sound.

The reason I have chosen these words is directly related to how they should be sung.

JUMPER: a pitched 'J' at the start of the word which moves on to the 'U' vowel. This can be sung well with a good breath, support from squeezing the *transversus abdominis* muscle in the lower stomach and an elongated 'U' vowel that is shaped the same as our previously rehearsed 'AAH' vowel. 'P' is an unvoiced consonant and so we simply make the sound and the 'ER' can be formed in the same way as the 'AAH' vowel.

CHAIR: 'CH' is an unpitched consonant sound, the rest of the word is formulated on the 'EH' vowel, with a slight use of diphthong (a combination of two vowels in which there is a noticeable sound change within the same syllable). We shall discuss diphthongs in the next section.

CLOTH: 'C' is an unvoiced consonant, 'L' is voiced, so pitched and then attached quickly to the 'OH' vowel, and 'TH' is an unpitched consonant sound. 'TH' must have enough airflow behind it to be sounded firmly and with intent so that this quite soft consonant sound carries across to anyone listening.

CLOTHED: 'C' is an unvoiced consonant 'L' is a voiced consonant and should be pitched and then attached quickly to the 'OH' vowel but the 'TH-E-D' is a pitched consonant sound followed by an open vowel. This is best sounded as a small diphthong in the voice so sounds like 'TH-UH', after which we simply add the unpitched 'D' consonant, so the last part of the word sounds as 'OH-TH-UH-D-UH'. Using this short diphthong before the D and after it helps round off the word well in pronunciation.

VOICED: I chose this word because of its ending. However, a V consonant is unvoiced. For it to carry well, its sound is best hardened almost akin to an 'F' sound (another unvoiced consonant!). The 'OH' should be well rounded but in this instance we must create another small diphthong-effect and run to sounds into each other – 'FV-OH-EE', the 'C' is an 'S' sound, so is unpitched and must be allowed to sound firmly. The '-ED' end of this word does not sound quite the same as 'CLOTHED', — it is a much harder sounding 'D' and sounded as a 'T'. So, the whole word is best sung as 'FV-OH-EE-S-T-UH-, with that extra little diphthong creeping in at the of the 'T' sound to round off the word correctly.

The celebrated American choral conductor, Robert Shaw, referred to the neutral vowel sound placed after a consonant as a 'schwa'; he particularly emphasized the need for this practice following or between plosives (explosive consonants).[1]

Eliding Consonants

In our everyday speaking, we have become skilled at short-cutting sounds to communicate faster. As a result, we run consonant sounds into one another and still communicate well. This deliberate (or perhaps subconscious) omission of sounds like consonants is called elision. Here are some everyday examples of when we elide our consonants:

Fish and chips = fish 'n' chips, gonna = going to, innit? = isn't it?

Elision of consonants in singing does not help with clarity, diction, or the rhythm of the text. Here are some examples of two phrases where the elision happens naturally. However, if we were singing these phrases, the elision should be taken away:

---

[1] Blocker, R. The Robert Shaw Reader, Yale Press, 2004

'That taketh' — spoken quickly becomes thataketh — if singing expect to hear both t's — That-uh Taketh

'Thus saith' — spoken quickly becomes thusaith — if singing expect to hear both s's — Thus-uh Saith

The examples here (taken from Händel and Mendelssohn) are in old-fashioned English, but we find elision in most choral music. Elision should be avoided, while forming the fullness of words and phrases should be encouraged.

Rules for singing consonants
We have some helpful rules in singing consonants, they are:

- All consonants should be supported by breath, like all our singing. Harder consonants may need a squeeze of the *transversis abdominis* muscle (the deepest of the 6 abdominal muscles)
- Unvoiced consonants cannot be shied away from, they are generally percussive and the noise they make is designed to carry so we can distinguish them. So don't try to dampen them, let them sound as they should
- Voiced consonants can be 'attached' or sung quickly into a following vowel. 'Holding on' to a consonant can create unnecessary vocal tension
- Softer voiced consonants such as 'TH' in 'CLOTHED' benefit from tucking in a small diphthong after them so that the sound carries. Unvoiced consonants at the ends of words benefit from the same approach but with a breath diphthong rather than a pitched 'UH' one
- Elision should be avoided at all costs for the sake of clarity, diction, and rhythm.

Diphthongs

A diphthong is a vowel sound that sounds like one sound bite but is made up of two distinct vowels seamlessly spoken or sung together. A good example of this is the word 'now'. If you say that word out loud, it sounds like one continuous sound but is, in fact, made up of 'Nah-ooh' — two vowel sounds together. Diphthongs are created for a unique sound in a word that we can differentiate aurally from other combinations of words and sounds. It is important therefore, to remember that diphthongs must be used well in singing to ensure that our words are properly rounded and sounded. Here are some examples of the eight most common diphthong sounds.

The two vowels sounded in the words:

'GOWN' – AH-OO
'PLIGHT' – AH-EE
'CLAY' – EH-EE
'STEER' – EE-UH
'SHOW' – O-OO
'PLOY' -O-EE
'SURE' – OO-UH

The International Phonetic Alphabet

The IPA was created in the 19th Century by the International Phonetic Association and was based primarily on Latin script. It is the standardized representation of the speech sounds we have been discussing here – in written form.

The symbols can represent two possible sounds – either: the sound of the letter in English or: the sound of the letter in English accompanied by a diacritic.[2]

---

[2] A diacritic is a mark, sign or accent appended to a letter in order to change its sound value and may appear above or below the letter itself

International Phonetic Alphabet Sounds In Everyday Speech

SHORT VOWELS

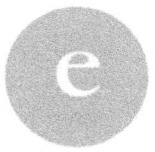

Went, intend, send, letter.

Cat, hand, nap, flat, have.

Fun, love, money, one, London, come.

Put, look, should, cook, book, look.

Rob, top, watch, squat, sausage.

Alive, again, mother.

LONG VOWELS

Need, beat, team.

Nurse, heard, third, turn.

Talk, law, bored, yawn, jaw.

Few, boot, lose, gloomy, fruit, chew.

Fast, car, hard, bath

The vital thing to remember about using diphthongs is that both vowels should be sounded. Best practice is to think of the two vowels with differing lengths; long followed by short. So, in the example of the word 'GOWN" the 'AAH' would be sounded just a little longer than the 'OOH' of 'G-AAH-OOH-N' — and to finish the word off well, we might add a small diphthong like sound to the -N' at the end, so the whole word sounds like this: -G-AAH-OOH-N-UH'. Try adding those sounds into your pronunciation of the word 'GOWN'. When you get used to all these extra sounds, we can use, recall, or look at the music for a current piece of repertoire that we are rehearsing and start examining the vowels, consonants, and diphthongs within our personal learning time on the music. If we start sounding the text properly, we will inspire others to do the same. Don't be surprised if other singers are impressed enough to ask how you are doing it because they want to develop this aspect of their singing. As a conductor, be prepared to spend some time on it during rehearsals — even better, plan to do so in your rehearsal schedule.

Chapter 6: Exercises for Vowels, Consonants and Diphthongs

Vowels and consonants are the sounds that make up our words. Each word can be carefully created with breath support, intent of breath, crisp clean consonants (voiced or unvoiced), diphthongs where necessary to create those tricky textual colours we are so used to in speech without dispensing with musicality and taking care of lazy or natural elision. Here are some samples of exercises to help with vowel placement, consonant placing and diphthong use.

Open Vowels Placement

1.

Exercise 1. Open vowels placement

- The rests should be used to give singers enough time to prepare an adequate breath for sustaining the open vowel sound
- Dynamics used should be at the conductor's discretion, but variable dynamics should be experimented with
- To maintain breath support, crescendo might be employed for each note.

2.

Open Vowel Words

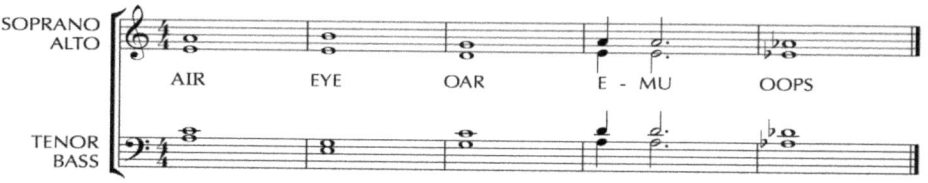

Exercise 2. Open vowel words

- The exercise might be run with breath marks after each semibreve or by seeking good elision by setting the breathing after every other semibreve
- Care over the timing and shaping of vowels in a uniform fashion should be taken
- The exercise can also be used to aid blending.

3.

Open Vowels Exercise 3

Created by: ERHarry

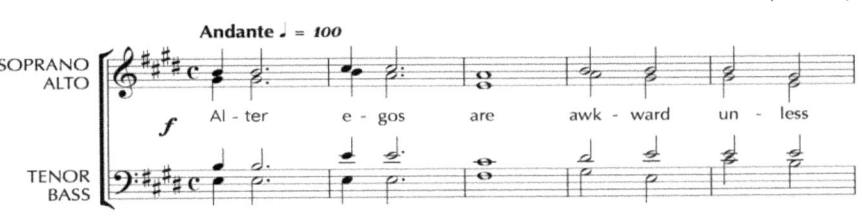

Exercise 3. Open vowels

- Breathing places should be established
- Singers should be careful with blending
- The tenor line is high and should be treated as the 'focal voice' with which to blend.

Placing Consonants

1.

Consonant Placing Exercise

Created by: ERHarry

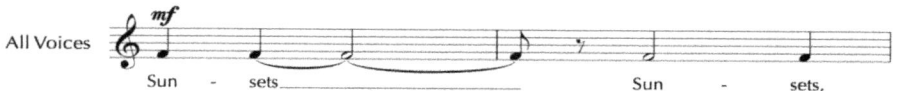

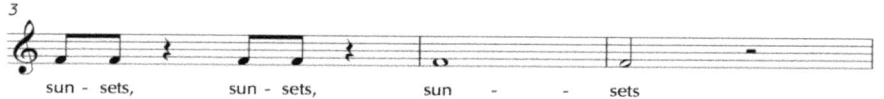

Exercise 1. Consonant placing exercise

- The exercise is written for all voices in unison
- Although there is a nominal dynamic, more specific dynamics could be added
- The exercise should be tried with different tempi.

2.

Parachute
- consonant placement exercise

Exercise 2. Consonants Placing

- Although based on a single word, the key element here is the timing of the syllables together, whilst listening to the other parts
- Dynamics can be changed to increase or decrease or remain the same
 throughout
- The exercise could be done in quartets, octets, or small groups, with each voice part selecting a dynamic of their own, increasing the need for the others to listen carefully.

Bing, Dm, Chee, Gn
(consonant exercise)

Created by: ERHarry

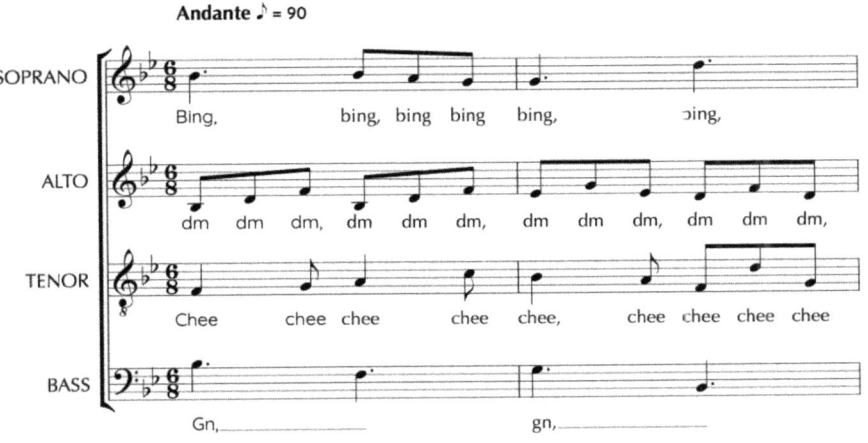

Exercise 3. Consonants

- These are closed consonant sounds which demand careful listening
- The singers will need to place the sounds carefully to achieve good timing
- Dynamics are at the discretion of the conductor.

Practising Vowels and Consonants

Short Exercise for Vowels & Consonants

Created by: ERHarry

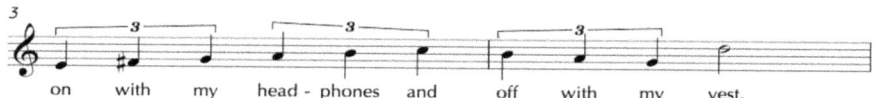

Exercise 1. Vowels and consonants

- The exercise for unison voices
- Care should be taken to ensure the minims are sounded correctly
- The triplets are a useful reminder for rhythmic purposes.

Positioning Diphthongs

Short Exercise for Diphthongs

Exercise 1. Diphthongs 1
- The attention needed here is on how the diphthong sounds change in all voices
- Although the tempo is set at *andante* there is no reason why the exercise could not be sung through at a slower speed, initially
- The placement of the consonants at the end of system 2 and 3 should be on the rests.

Diphthongs 2

Created by: ERHarry

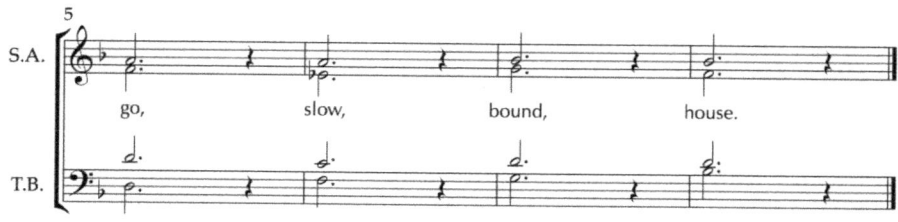

Exercise 2. Diphthongs 2

- Isolated diphthong words for careful shaping in four parts
- The choir will need to listen to itself and watch for any cues from the conductor
- One syllable words are easier to use to help isolate the diphthong action needed.

Random Diphthongs 3

Created by: ERHarry

Exercise 3. Diphthongs 3

- Diphthong sounds in relation to more than one note
- Isolate one system at a time as necessary to work on the uniform shaping of the diphthongs
- Breathing on the punctuation.

The work needed on training a choir to become aware of listening to its own consonant and diphthong placement can be intense and may feel laborious, but it will pay in dividends. Where possible it might be worth planning the work in this area so that it becomes a part of your working schedule and generally part of your choir's development.

Chapter 7: Listening Exercises – Pairs or Small groups and the Whole Choir

Working on developing singers' ability to listen with others is a profitable way to spend some rehearsal (and social!) time together away from the rehearsal room itself. A good conductor will always encourage choir members to spend time together working on the music and bonding socially.

Our singing voices are a very personal part of who we are. We can communicate how we are feeling through vocal music. We can expose our sensitive and emotional sides. We can also expose our vocal habits and blemishes that are easier to hide in amongst the choir. Feeling able to sing in front of another person requires some trust and confidence that the other person will not judge too critically how we sound. The same can be said for working in small groups of three or four.

Working in pairs or small groups give the opportunity to listen to voices individually, handing out hints and tips and to go over notes made during a formal rehearsal. If your group has experienced and confident singers, meeting up with members of other sections to develop their listening skills or rehearse in harmony can be very rewarding. If singers are less confident about their singing or recall of the music from the rehearsal, getting together with members of the same voice section will be helpful.

The following exercises can be done in pairs or small groups and may seem basic at first, but the skills you'll develop will show in any subsequent rehearsals.

Pair or Small Group Exercises

Humming

Sit with your partner or small group and simply hum the same note together. As you sit and hum the same pitch, listen to each other's voices. Are they the same volume? Is one louder or softer than the other? Aim to make an even sound between you, regardless of how many voices are humming in the room. This can take time but the more you do this, the more you will become attuned to when you have found that even tone between you. When you can do this at one volume, try and set yourselves the task of doing the same at varying dynamics. Don't be afraid to go louder than *mezzo piano* or *piano*.

Pitching and Rhythm

This pitching and rhythm exercise can then be extended to include small musical phrases if you feel creative. To start, decide on a singing order within your group. The first person sings a note (for example, using the syllable 'lah') and everyone else repeats it. You then go round the room — or bounce between you if in pairs — aiming to pitch back the exact given note. Quicken the tempo as you go and see how quickly you can hear and then repeat the pitch back. To concentrate on rhythm only, try the same exercise but repeat a clapped rhythm — which can be more challenging.

Scalic Work

Sing some simple scales together in the mid-range of your voices, perhaps using 'Doh-Re-Mi-Fa-Soh-Lah-Ti-Doh.' Vary the starting pitch and tempo.

When you've done this a few times, try singing the same scales with one or more of you starting and returning to the top of the scale, whilst the other starts and returns to the bottom. Again, listen to each other and stay in time with each other.

When you are effortlessly singing the scales simultaneously, try a standard version of the scale where (if in pairs) you only sing alternate notes to each other, like this:

Person A:	**Person B:**
Doh	
	Re
Mi	
	Fah
Soh	
	Lah
Ti	
	Doh

Then reverse it or include more than the standard eight notes of the scale, then try it backwards. The aim is to set up a flowing tempo and see if you can sing the scales divided between you seamlessly, as if with one voice. Speed it up, slow it down until it works between you.

Lip Syncing

Sit facing one another and decide what you are going to sing. For this exercise, something very familiar is best. Suggestions might include 'Happy Birthday', a national anthem, a nursery rhyme or hymn or even a round or a folk song. Once decided, face each other and sing it together. As you do this, look at each other's mouths. The aim is to shape and mouth the words simultaneously or 'in sync' with each other, so your voices are perfectly matched in tempo, diction and text delivery. It's not as easy to get complete accuracy as you might think! When you can do this with a couple of well-known songs or pieces of music, try it with a passage from the repertoire you are working on with the choir.

Listening and Syncing with Closed Eyes

Sit or stand with your partner or the group facing you but not too close. Choose one of you to 'lead', then, close your eyes. The person leading will breathe in and start singing a pre-decided piece of music. The aim of this exercise is for all to sing together, stay in tempo with the leader, and keep the same dynamics and articulation but with your eyes closed. By closing your eyes, you will be wholly reliant on listening to the leader to stay in sync. The leader should choose a piece of music known to the pair or group but is not too short. The whole group should concentrate on singing and breathing together just by listening.

Back-to-Back

Sit back-to-back with your partner or sit up close with your group, at back-to-back angles. Be careful to sit facing away from each other. Sitting back-to-back is crucial for this exercise as you need to feel when the other person is breathing in. Start singing a pre-decided piece of music and learn to inhale in and out sync with the others, as you feel breaths through your back. Keep the singing in tune, in time and in sync by listening carefully. It's more difficult when the person leading is facing away from you, but this exercise is good training for the rehearsal room as it forces you to listen to someone singing who is neither side of you and so the sound is more difficult hear — a bit like trying to listen to the Bass section sing if you are at the opposite end of the room and singing Soprano.

Whole Choir Exercises

The following exercises are designed for the whole choir and are best done during the warm-up period in the rehearsal room:

Silence

Silence is a fascinating thing — a whole choir making no noise of their own volition, just listening to the noises they can hear naturally occurring inside and outside of the room. Listening is a discipline we don't often embrace for several reasons — isn't it a waste of time? What happens if someone's phone or smart watch rings or chimes with a message alert? Silence can induce mild anxiousness in some people, who like regular noise and feel awkward by complete silence.

Having a short period of silence just to listen can help focus our attention away from the outside world and toward the rehearsal and its demands. In fact, making space in your warm-up for a period of silence may help your choir be more at ease, relaxed and ready to sing with better attention. Creating a period of silence in your warm-up requires the co-operation of everyone. Tell them to switch off their mobile devices, stop trying to find the right music, sit or stand in a relaxed way and close their eyes or focus on one single point in the room. If a choir can find its 'silence', it can use this to great advantage in its music-making.

It might be an obvious thing to say, but there is silence before every piece of music. In that silence, a musician focuses before starting to play a solo, a singer relaxes and breathes to be ready to sing, and members of the orchestra concentrate on getting their fingers or mouths into the first position to play an opening passage or introduction.

Choirs must learn to find their silence in the rehearsal room — to 'revisit' their silent mode — before beginning a performance and when they come to the end of a piece. If there is a keyboard or other instrumental introduction, the choir should 'find their silence' before they start singing. Good conductors will allow their singers to relax, prepare internally and focus on the music in hand by allowing time in silence before singing.

The art of choral silence is a truly fascinating one; there are, after all, silences within music and, therefore, during performances and rehearsals. One might say that silence is music, therefore. If a choir can create that silent mode and practices that silence, they should be able to recreate that silence on almost any given rest in the music. Silence becomes a rehearsed part of the music and, in doing so, the relaxation, inner preparation and focus that goes with 'silent mode' is translated into the rehearsal and performance of a piece. This, in turn, means that singers do not lose focus during periods of rest when singing, remain relaxed and are continually preparing for their next entry. Do your choir members write in the number of beats rest they have in their scores? Ask them to do this habitually — it will result in less analysis and more time to listen to what is going on around them.

Dynamic Isolation

Invariably, choral dynamics can be quite generous in volume. They can also be a bit 'hit and miss' and are often inconsistent: a *piano* in a piece of music by Brahms may not necessarily be the same *piano* sound in a piece by Bach, Haydn, or Parry. To avoid these inconsistencies, 'setting up' dynamic sounds for a choir is an important journey to embark upon.

For the following exercises, it's best to use something familiar to the choir.

Rehearse a small section of music and ask them to carefully use the dynamics written in the score to create the piece as accurately as possible.

Then, in the case of a *piano* marking, isolate where this dynamic starts and stops, and rehearse it again asking the choir to carefully listen to the sound and volume they are creating together. Now, choose another *piano* section in the same piece and ask the choir to sing it. Is it the same sound and volume as the first extract? If not, why not? They need to understand how consistency of dynamic helps create even tone and even balance across the choir. It is worth regularly practising 'dynamic isolation' exercises with the choir; a choir evolves when it learns that it must be able to identify its own *pianissimo* to *fortissimo* graded sounds. Every choir is unique in this regard. A choir must 'own' its dynamics, be able to identify when they are singing either too softly or too loudly for the marked dynamic direction and be able to self-regulate. This process creates a degree of autonomy for the choir over its own dynamics, which is a healthy development as it means the choir is listening and adapting as it goes along.

Quartets

Another good exercise for improve the choir's listening is to ask members not to sit in their voice sections but to form discrete quartets with members of the other three voice section (or however many other parts you have in your choir). It should be noted that this exercise won't work if the choir is in the early stages of learning a piece of repertoire but instead will work when everyone is more comfortable and confident with what they are singing. The members should form quartets and sit or stand in them — it helps if they form small circles of their own as a foursome. Then, rehearse the piece with everyone singing their part. Was it successful? Could the singers keep to their parts when they heard the other three parts more closely? Some singers will feel flummoxed at first and so it is worth running the exercise two or three times. When the choir returns to sitting in their vocal sections the following may occur:

- A sense of increased confidence in the vocal parts
- An over-generous dynamic because of the point above
- The choir's overall sensitivity to the other parts may well improve.

Mirrored Vowels

This exercise is fun but can be slightly chaotic. First, give each member their own individual vowels to sing by handing them a piece of paper with that vowel on. Ask them to keep their vowel a secret. When the choir has been given their vowels, ask them to pitch any note and sing their vowel, stopping when they run out of breath and 'returning to the sound' on a new breath. Now, the members should move around the room trying to find those who are also singing the same vowel. The successful groups will be those who are clearly shaping their vowels correctly and can easily identify them by listening.

Posture

Many things affect our listening, and the chances are that if we display a rather over-relaxed attitude in our physical form, then our listening has also become too relaxed. It is important to emphasise the need for good posture when singing — whether that is sitting down or standing up. Posture plays a key part in helping us sing in a healthy way and whilst this book is not about posture, remind your choir that where posture goes, all other disciplines follow — including listening.

'Ear' Training

There are many ways to help train your choir's ears so that the singers become attuned to one another whilst singing. For example, by asking them to identify major and minor chords on the keyboard or piano or time signatures from a piece played to them. To start, play the root note of a chord (C for C Major or Minor) and ask the choir to sing the rest of the chord according to their voice part. This may need demonstrating for those who are not accustomed to music theory. Once the choir successfully creates major chords above each root note, ask them to produce minor chords — then seventh chords and even suspended chords. Again, some of this may need explaining and demonstrating before attempting it.

Another useful exercise is asking the choir to sing a chord and then move the pitch up or down, a semitone at a time. When the choir finishes the exercise, is it in tune with the original chord that was set up?

Take the Conductor Away

One of the possible issues with having a conductor (please note we need conductors!) is that a choir can become over-reliant on someone gesturing musical interpretation, emphasising beats and or mouthing the text (this is not good practice!) at the choir. To regain the balance between autonomy and being conducted, ask the choir to sing without a piano introduction or conducting gestures. This may not work successfully the first time but if attempted for a second or third time, it won't be long before music 'happens by itself' and the choir sing it together without the conductor.

Another option is for the conductor to start off with the choir and then to stop conducting altogether, allowing the choir to sing through the piece without gestures or beats in front of them. This will reveal how many members have made notes on the musical direction asked for, who is confident singing their part and who is reading and executing the correct dynamics.

Lights Out

If your choir rehearses in the evening and it is the autumn or winter season, try asking the members to sing together in the dark – with the lights off. This is a 'shortcut' to achieving greater listening discipline as darkness helps to magnify sounds. Choir members can hear more easily when individual voices sing outside an established dynamic. It allows them to listen closely to themselves breathing together, phrasing the beginnings and endings of words together. This exercise also induces greater intimacy as the visual distractions of the room vanish and the choir sound is heard more keenly. Sadly, those effects may dissipate when the lights are switched back on, but it is worth highlighting how heightened listening can be achieved in darkness.

Chapter 8: Exercises: General, Elision, Listening

General

**Unison Octave
Placements Exercise**

Created by: ERHarry

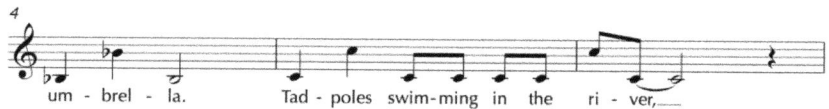

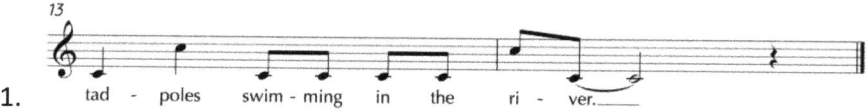

Exercise 1. Unison octave placement

Car Manufacturer
(placement exercise for vowels & consonants)

Created by: ERHarry

As well as shaping the mouth and soft palate correctly for successful octave intervals, the shaping of vowels should also be given attention.

Exercise 2. Vowel and consonants placement

Run the exercise as written, ask the singers to place the 'schwa' or neutral vowel after each consonant, on the following rests.

Symbiotic Revellry
- warm up with consonants, vowels and diphthongs

Created by: ERHarry

Varying Tempi

All Voices

Sym - bi - o - tic rev - el - lry.

Sym - bi - o - tic rev - el - lry.

etc..

Exercise 3. Warm up for consonants, vowels, and diphthongs

As it only uses the first five notes of a major scale it can be repeated, rising by a semitone each time, from any starting pitch, to cover most of the vocal ranges

Elision

Elision - Exercise 1

Exercise 1. Elision 1

- Nonsense words easy to 'run in' to each other
- Emphasise how words can be elided and the effect of elision on clarity and diction
- Dynamics may be varied as appropriate.

Elision - Exercise 2
(TTBB)

Created by: ERHarry

Elision - 2
(SATB)

Created by: ERHarry

Exercise 2. Elision 2

- Diphthongs are used in this exercise in mostly single syllable words
- The punctuation used to help with clarity and diction

Toasted Teacakes
(Elision 1)

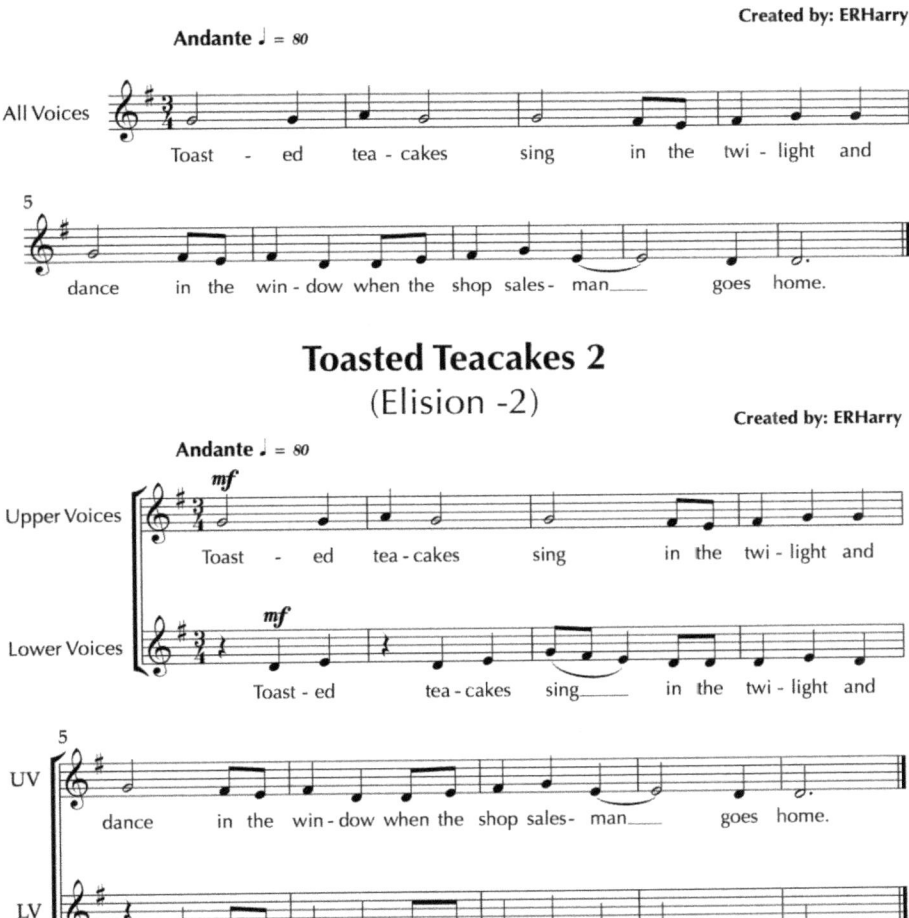

Toasted Teacakes 2
(Elision -2)

Exercise 3. Elision 3

- **'Toasted Teacakes 2'** is an exercise for the choir to work on split into upper and lower voices who must listen to one another and successfully place their consonant sounds together as a result

Listening

Can You Hear Me Calling?

Exercise 1. Listening

- Basses set the dynamic each time and the other parts follow (if they are listening!)
- 'Question & Answer' exercise designed to get singers listening to each other
- The final 'far away!' is in unison; singers should aim to blend their sound for this.

MAH
- a short exercise in dynamics

Created by: ERHarry

Exercise 2. Dynamics

- The dynamics are in charge in this exercise, getting it correct according to what is written requires practice!

Phrasing and Answering Exercise

The sections should seamlessly run into one another as if in 'one voice'.

Working on the placement of syllables, consonants and elision can feel like 'microscopic detail' at times but developing exercises to include in your warm-ups will focus the learning and re-learning of such skills early on in rehearsals and the investment will pay off as the choir begin to listen to the effect of success on their overall sound. Conductors are then able to refer to the warm-up exercises used when working on elements such as these.

Chapter 9: Blending

Food blenders are a wonderful creation. By plugging them into an electric source, they will mix any number of ingredients you add in a much faster way than a hand by hand with a spoon. The result of the electric blender is almost always a more consistent and well-blended food mix. The manual method can often leave some sections of the mix less well blended.

There is a direct correlation between the food blender and the need for a choir to sing with a *unified* sound. Choirs aspire to have a 'unified sound' when working together to re-create written music from the page (though singing from memory is wonderfully releasing when possible!). But how do we achieve choral blend as singers and conductors? This chapter offers good advice on how to achieve the best choral blend. It is not designed to have all the answers but offers things to think about when aiming for the best unified sound possible. Later, it also discusses the less often used voice-blending approach by voice type.

Why Does a Choir Need to Blend?

A choir is a group of people who enjoy singing together, whether during rehearsals or in public. They want to belong to a group of like-minded individuals and share and believe in its values and ethos. Members of a choir give up their individualism to contribute to singing as a whole learning their text and vocal part to create choral music. For some, it is a pastime, for others it is a way of life and a career. In any case, joining a choir should bring much joy and energy to its participants. However, when individual voices can be heard above the general sound of the choir and are identifiable to anyone listening, it creates an uneven or unbalanced sound and the focus of anyone listening is taken away from the effect of the whole choir. If, as a member of the choir, you are either sitting or standing next to the person who sounds much louder or different than everyone else, it might be a negative experience as a strident voice can be intimidating, off-putting or stopping you from listening to anything else. We will discuss how to manage people who either have difficulty with or refusing to blend later. For now, it should be noted that a choir with individual voices sticking out is no longer a choir, it's a group of individuals who just happen to be singing the same piece.

Helping Your Choir to blend

There are some basic ingredients that help a choir to blend, some of which have been discussed in previous chapters. However, it is worth reminding ourselves of those basic elements before we discuss things in further depth:

Vocal volume. The volume at which we sing is changeable, however, singers must remember to remain sensitive to their volume and the volume of others when they sing together. Ask your singers to sing and to listen to those close to them. This can instantly resolve some blending issues. Listening can be the first discipline to be neglected, and so early on in a rehearsal session (and then every so often throughout) remind singers to listen to their singing neighbours and to compare their volume with the volume of those around them.

Rhythm and timing. During a rehearsal, particularly if there is a need to complete a rehearsal schedule, it is easy for either singers or conductors to gloss over the fact that there may be rhythmic or timing errors during the first learning session of a piece of music. Rhythm and timing are essential for helping with a choral blend, they are also essential for good diction and clarity and so it is advantageous to tackle incorrectly interpreted rhythms and timings immediately. That may seem overly fussy in the early stages of the rehearsal of a piece, but if we allow ourselves to rehearse incorrectly, it might be that those incorrect rhythms or timings become 'set' and then difficult to re-learn.

Vowels and consonants. Vowels and consonants are the nuts and bolts of the text we sing. We must rehearse to sing the words clearly and together, whether that togetherness is per voice section or per the whole choir. This, of course, helps with the overall blend of the choir. Straggling ends of phrases, stray hard consonants (like s and t for example) and variations in the pronunciation of certain words all detract from the overall vocal effectiveness of the choir — the effectiveness of its blend.

Good vocal technique (GVT). This is trickier. A good choral conductor will be able to instruct with knowledge and understanding around the topic of vocal technique, to help train the choir to sing properly. If this is not a specialist subject for a conductor, sessions with vocal coaches may be appropriate to consider. Suffice it to say that all members of a choir are happy to receive vocal training to help better themselves and benefit the choir as a whole. GVT should include instruction on breath support, the correct use of a breath, tips on various aspects of the vocal mechanism (laryngeal area and surrounding muscles) and using the mouth, lips, tongue, teeth and palates correctly for singing.

Vocal tone for interpretation. Interpreting different types of music may well require the choir to change the general tone of the sound it produces. For example, a dynamic marking *piano legato espressivo* should sound different from a *piano agitato*. So that these vocal effects are managed well, choirs need to regularly use warm up and other vocal exercises to create these differing sounds. They are a change from the every-day tone of natural singing, and we should, therefore, rehearse these too so that they are not unusual sounds to us when called upon to insert them into a piece.

Vocal tone for blend. Concentrate on how the singing voices sound compared with the others around them. Are the singers singing with a rasp? Breathily? Too loudly? With too much vibrato? Ahead of the beat? Ahead of others in the section? Behind? With correct or incorrect rhythm? Do their diction, diphthongs, vowels, consonants sound the same as others? Is vocal tension being created as they sing? And can you, as conductor, spot this in your singers?

Listening and intonation. Intonation is the 'tuning in' of the sound made by the choir to ensure that the singing voices are in the same pitch or key as either an accompanying instrument or the other voices around them. Horizontal intonation is the ability to listen, hear and adjust your own tuning. Our bodies are not designed to hear our voices as others hear them and so this takes time to develop but we can be helped and supported by vertical intonation — listening to others around us and the accompanying instrument to keep our pitching 'in sync'. We can understand therefore, how listening as a discipline is the root of all that is good about singing chorally. We'll discuss intonation with tone later in this chapter as we explore voice types and voice type blending.

Non-Blenders: An Approach

Despite a conductor's clear instructions, there are times when individual choir members simply do not remember that they are part of a collective and should be blending into the sound. The phenomenon of non-blending is not uncommon and can be off-putting to those choir members who must endure sitting or standing next to someone insensitive to the rest of the sound being created in the room.

There are also occasions when a particular singer wishes to be heard in a prevalent way. I can instantly think of several members of choirs past and present whom I have directed, whose voices stood out for a period of time.

Non-blending singing cannot be ignored and there are several ways to tackle it. The first is quite brutal: direct conversation with the individual involved. It is possible that the singer is unaware that they are not blending or, it could be that the singer feels they know the material and that they have taken it upon themselves to 'lead' the voice section in learning. In this latter situation, you can thank the singer for the 'selfless act' of helping their section but then ask them not to do it anymore — to avoid the section becoming reliant on one person leading the voice part. This should be effective because you've acknowledged their hard work but also asked for it to stop. If it happens again however, just point out that you can hear an individual voice coming through. If it continues, it is worth speaking to the individual concerned again, but this time with someone else present — perhaps a member of a managing committee or another member of the music team. There have been rare occasions where I have been left with no further alternative other than to address the individual by name, in the rehearsal, in front of all present. This has always been a very last resort as it can be both difficult and embarrassing — but it does stop this from happening.

Blending Exercises

Conductors should take the listening approach when running blending exercises with their choir. Ask the choir members to form a circle — depending on the size of your choir it is OK to have a circle more than one person deep. On forming a circle, the choir should simply sing what they have been rehearsing. If they have previously been seated in a 'concert-like' formation facing the front, this new shape will enable them to hear all the other parts much more easily and will help with blending.

Another version of this exercise is to ask each voice section to sit together in one of the corners of the room and then to ask each section to listen to one voice part at a time. This will change the way dynamics are sung as the singers try to listen to a voice part that is now further away. However, it will also even out the sound, as listening takes priority. If you are feeling particularly brave, you can ask each section to turn to face away from the room, so the listening really does have to take priority!

A final version of this exercise is to ask all members to go into the middle of the room (if it is safe to do so from a health and safety point of view), to look at each other and sing - ideally, with their eyes closed and to listen to all those voices close up. Then, as they sing, they should concentrate on allowing their voices to become 'less individual' and to 'find' a volume and tone where they all sound the same. If this is successful, singers should be asked to remember what that ultimate blend sounded like and to recall it when they sit in a normal rehearsal formation.

I've included some examples or 'starting points' for developing exercises to help with blending. These are found in chapter 10. It's best to develop unique exercises for your choir or group to sing together — those described in this book provide good starting points.

Voice Types

There is another way of helping to develop the blend of a choir. However, the process can be unsettling and controversial for singers unless it is explained clearly to them before it happens.

We are all aware that our voices are unique; Unique vocal markers vary and include:

- Individual pattern of speech
- Impediments
- Accent
- Whether the person is bilingual or multilingual
- Whether there are any medical implications for speech and singing
- The general shape and size of a person's mouth.

All these things can act as vocal markers for how the singing voice may ultimately sound. On top of this, there are different types of singing voices with different tone and timbre in this instance. Again, these are many and varied and I am sure you will be able to add your own but here is list of the types of voices that we may come across:

- Nasal
- Raspy
- Gruff
- Throaty
- Thin and reedy
- Breathy and quiet
- Overly *vibrato*
- Microtonally under the required pitch
- Generally sharper than the required pitch.

The list could go on. Please note that there is nothing negative about the qualities mentioned here. That is what is so exciting about singing in a choir — it can incorporate all voice types! The question is only, how?

A good method to help is to practise physical blending exercises with your choir. It is a general 'sorting' of who sits where in the choir and can be incorporated as part of a new conductor's strategy for blending – or for an established conductor to continue the work needed.

What is Voice Placement?

Physically blending your choir requires patience, sensitivity, experience, and people management skills. It should not be attempted by a newly qualified conductor, joining a choir for the first time. Physically blending the choir involves moving singers around until an as-even-as-possible tone is achieved purely by listening to and analysing the singing voices alone. It needs careful consideration and time to get to know the types of singing voices in the choir. By isolating certain sections of the choir and listening carefully to each singer, then moving them to match with another voice type that compliments both singers together, it is possible to create a more even tone. For example, by isolating a row of Basses and asking them to sing together, you'll hear their voices better. This way, you can ask the singers to move position until the voices are set in a way that compliments the overall sound as well as the individual voices, creating a more even tone. The singers should then adopt this new formation as 'set'. Should there be absences at rehearsal, those seats should remain empty and not be filled in until a good 15 minutes after the rehearsal has started.

Why would you do it?

There are a few reasons why physically blending the choir in this way is advantageous:
- It is possible to hear the individual voices more easily
- A more even tone is created and the section sounds better together as a result
- The exercises act as a subconscious request for the singers to listen to one another and to blend
- The processes can help stop individual singing voices or vocal issues becoming too apparent
- Other voice sections observing should begin to hear the difference 'before' and 'after' and be able to feed that back to themselves.

How and when to do it, sensitively

There is no fixed best time for physical blending and conductors need to be prepared for feedback from singers who are not happy to move position on a permanent basis because they are used to singing with their friends and neighbours in a particular formation. The best time to move singers is either at the very beginning of a contract of work, when nothing can be perceived as either biased or personal, or when conductors feel they have the trust and confidence of their choir. Avoid 'experiments' at all costs.

The listening and aural analysis skills to make this work, demand that the conductor can identify voice types that complement and match each other. Further, the 'people skills' required when asking singers to move from their seats in a supportive, encouraging and transparent way are advanced and come with experience. Conductors should be cautious if they intend to blend their choirs physically. It must be done with clear explanations, which are underlined repeatedly.

Developing the listening and aural analysis skills needed for such an exercise is a journey unto itself. Conductors can work on developing these skills in rehearsals. Conductors should ask themselves the following questions and establish the answers over time:

- Which voices remain individual after a blending exercise and why?
- Which are the weaker and stronger voices in every row of every section?
- Which group within a vocal section has an uneven tone?
- Which are the stronger music readers or quicker interpreters in each section — and which are the weaker?
- Will the weaker benefit if the stronger are directly behind, to the left, or right?

These are just some of the questions listening conductors could ask themselves.

What does voice placement achieve?

If physical blending is done accurately and the singers remember with whom they should now be sitting every week (and in a performance) it will aid the choir as a whole by:

- Evening the tone in every row of every voice section, with no individual voices sounding out
- Supporting those struggling with pitch or rhythm
- 'Soaking' up individual vocal issues
- Improving the overall sound of each voice section.

It is imperative that conductors become *au fait* with the voice types within the groups of singers they work with. They can then deduct how the voices can complement each other — their individual strengths and weaknesses and abilities. A lot of the preparatory work can be done by conductors simply listening to the voices before them. There is no doubt that the aims and objectives reflected upon here are only achievable by listening — and that is listening by the choir and by the conductor, as a two-way process — a team effort for the good of the whole choir.

Directional listening or 'zoning' your listening

As your listening practice develops you will become accustomed to identifying voice types
   (As previously mentioned in 'voice placement'), vocal zones, sectional strengths and weaknesses and vertical and horizontal grading and shading:

Voice Types

I previously mentioned examples of different voice types when discussing 'voice placement' earlier in the chapter. Those examples were:

- nasal
- raspy
- gruff
- throaty
- thin and reedy
- breathy and quiet
- overly vibrato
- microtonally (or more) under the required pitch
- generally sharper than the required pitch

To identify these voice types – and others – within a vocal ensemble, we must listen to the collection of voices singing. Take time to concentrate on one voice at a time, perhaps listening to those directly in front of you, then in the front and to the side. If it helps, move closer to those you want to listen to but in no way should a conductor make it overly obvious that they are listening to an individual; if it becomes apparent, the singer can be embarrassed or feel somewhat intimidated and won't sing as you need them to.

As you listen, identify the voice type you are listening to against either the list above, or your own list of descriptions. Identifying voices singing further away than the first couple of rows becomes easier if you ask voice sections to rehearse passages of music alone and standing up. You should end up with a 'vocal map' of all the voice types in the ensemble. When you have completed this, it becomes easier to manage the voices against the blending qualities of each type, for a smoother vocal sound and thus be able to seat them according to the best natural blending. This also removes the notion that voice placement is personal.

Zoning - vocal

With a 'voice type map' in place, the choir can be more easily divided into vocal zones of a certain number of singers. The question is, which voice types are complimentary with one another, and which do nothing to help with 'evening out' the general vocal tone and timbre through a seated line of singers? The exercise here is taking the time to try different combinations of voice types together. Listening carefully, the conductor should try 'matching' voices together experimentally. Conductors may be advised by starting with just two voices and then adding voices to this pair, to create full rows of 'matched' or 'even' voices singing together, in the voice section. Here's an example:

Loud/Confident.   Quiet.   Modest.   Nasal

When wishing to seat your singers in zones, perhaps a good way to start might be with the strongest voice being at the 'heart' of the zone and then matching the other voices around it. An example might look like this:

When considering a different row of singers, say the row in front of the group in the diagram, care should be taken to listen to where the strongest voices sit in relation to one another – too close and they may overpower a section, too far away and they may sound too 'individual' and unbalance the section. And so, the 'zones' may be considered to be both horizontal (by row) and vertical (by columns through the voice section):

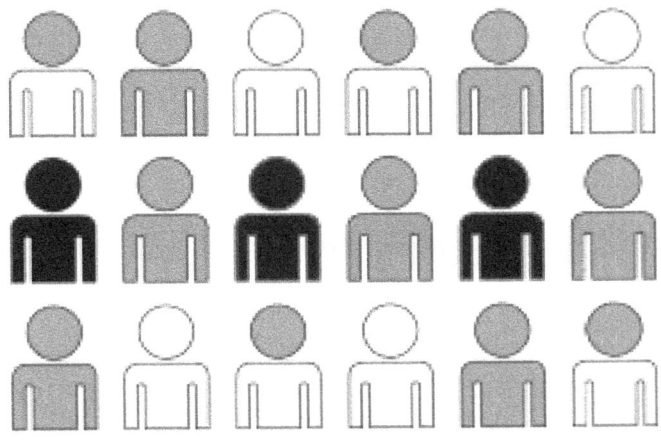

A possible horizonal/vertical scenario. Would this work for your choir?

Zoning the choir like this can help place voices correctly regardless of voice section and can help develop vocal sonority that is identifiable from within the choir itself. In other words, the singers themselves can recognise that being grouped in certain formations gives them confidence, colour, character and quality not previously attained. When the singers themselves can identify the advantages of vocal placement and zoning, they appreciate the exercise and understand its worth. The examples above are not set patterns of success so be prepared to work with your choir to find the right seating solution for it.

Zoning – listening

With voice placement and zoning exercises completed, it is now aurally easier to identify voice sections, groups of voices and vocal zones, when we listen. In other words, we are seating the singers to become more aurally accessible to us - as conductors -as we listen. Identifying and then becoming more familiar with the voices singing (as we go through voice placement exercises etc.) helps us to develop a deeper awareness with each individual voice, voices within small groups and voices within vocal zones. This, in turn, aids us as conductors to aurally identify individuals, small groups and zones within the general ensemble and helps us 'zone in' our listening. The ensemble, regardless of size is now designed in more manageable 'zones', which can be notated, if necessary; the vocal sound is now more organised to our aural advantage which helps us do the job better – as well as naturally aiding the choir in blending better. We can now identify sections that are making errors in rehearsals, ill-formed vowels, consonants etc.. breathing preparation, dynamic control etc. quickly and efficiently and address these.

Sectional Strengths and Weaknesses

As part of vocal placement exercises, vocal sonority within whole voice sections (Soprano, Alto, Tenor, Bass etc.) will have gained strength and consistency. It is now worth considering how the vocal sections themselves manage these new formations to achieve an even higher standard of vocal blend. Following the creation of a new seating plan, formed from voice type identification and then achieving best timbral consistency through voice placement and vocal zoning, conductors or vocal coaches should find time to work through exercises to help 'settle the sectional sound'. Voice placements and zoning can be an unsettling affair for a choir, particularly if some singers have been sitting together for a long time. Ensuring that support through these possible changes is continued, sections now need to work through their vocal strengths and weaknesses together in what might be a changed formation. Conductors should be careful to be encouraging and actively engaging with each voice section to build confidences.

Vertical and Horizontal vocal gradation

The most common form of listening, when identifying or comparing voice types is horizontal in nature – the act of putting voices together in a row, for the most consistent vocal tone. This is an act of aural gradation for the benefit and advantage of the singers and whole vocal ensemble.

Conductors should also consider vertical gradation during the process of developing voice placements and listening to voice types.

The vertical version of such a listening process is considering which voices are placed behind - or in front of - which, and whether this has either a wanted or unwanted effect on the vocal sonority of the ensemble. For example, it might be that through the process of elimination, the most advantageous, horizontal seating arrangements have been found for the Tenor section (for example) of a chamber choir, however when the Tenors are placed in the back row of the new formation, they naturally begin to deliver 'louder than previous' dynamics or entries that sound 'behind the beat'; this is because they are at the back and naturally feel the need to project their sound over the (for example) Altos sitting in front of them.

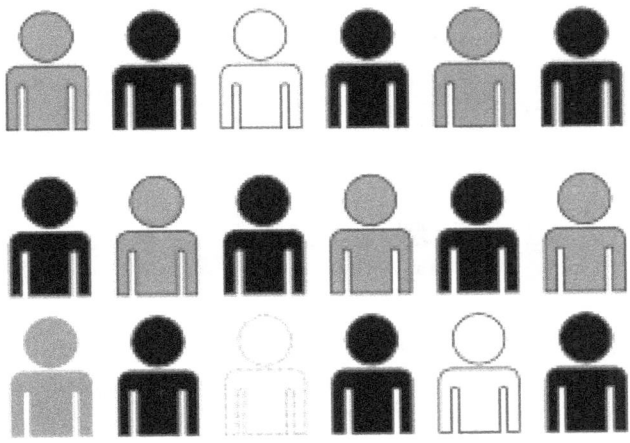

Therefore, the formation of the choir now needs to be addressed from a 'vertical listening' point of assessment. Every ensemble might have a unique way of sitting that best delivers a sonorous, consistent and well-balanced sound and conductors should support the choir in finding that most advantageous of formations.

Chapter 10: Exercises — Blending, Rhythm, Syllabic Placement

Blending

Exercise 1. Blending

- Syllabic exercise for listening to and blending the vowels, as well as listening for an overall blend and consistent consonant placement
- The exercise should be run on one dynamic only and not with extreme dynamics.

Humming Exercise
(helps with listening to blend)

Created by: ERHarry

Exercise 2. Humming
- The key to this exercise is listening well enough to find the correct balance for all parts to be heard successfully
- The exercise should be run on one dynamic only — *mezzo piano* or another dynamic.

Blending Exercise
- using vowels (Italianate)

Created by: ERHarry

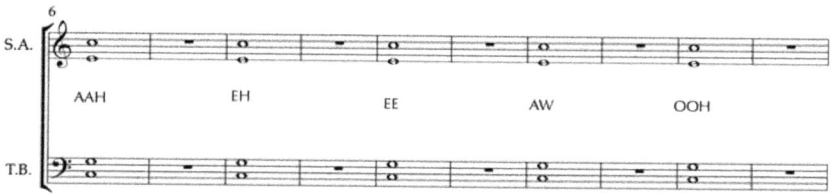

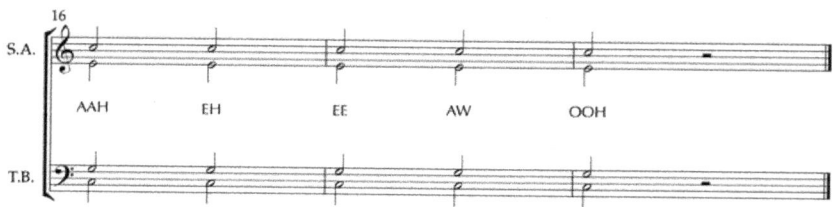

Exercise 3. Blending vowels

- This exercise should be done slowly, allowing enough time for the choir to listen to the sound for each vowel, giving time for the listening to improve the blend
- *Crescendi* can be introduced once the sounds have blended effectively, and the choir acknowledged the blended sound for each vowel.

Rhythm

Exercise 1. Rhythm
- Constructed to challenge elision and the placing of the 'ng' sound
- Unison voices exercise
- Worth learning this 'by rote' and then changing the starting note to cover more of the vocal ranges.

Ding Dong!

Created by: ERHarry

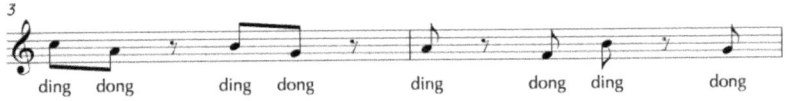
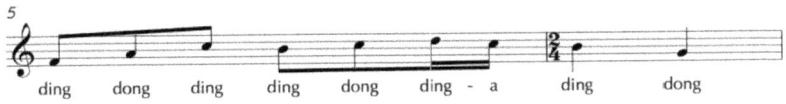

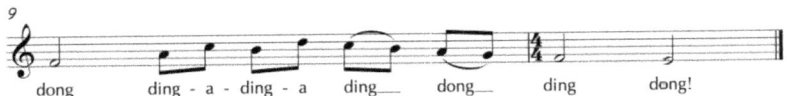

Exercise 2. More rhythm

- Constructed to challenge elision and the placing of the consonant sounds
- For unison voices
- Choose different starting pitches to cover more of the vocal ranges
- Use one dynamic at a time.

Swirling Ribbons

Created by: ERHarry

All Voices

Swirl-ing rib-bons, grunt-ing gib-bons, smi - ling and yawn ing in the

dawn - ing yel-low sun, a box full of chocs for my tea.

Exercise 3. More rhythm

- Unison voices exercise
- Consonant sounds should be placed uniformly.

Syllables
Cheeseburgers and Chocolate Ice Cream

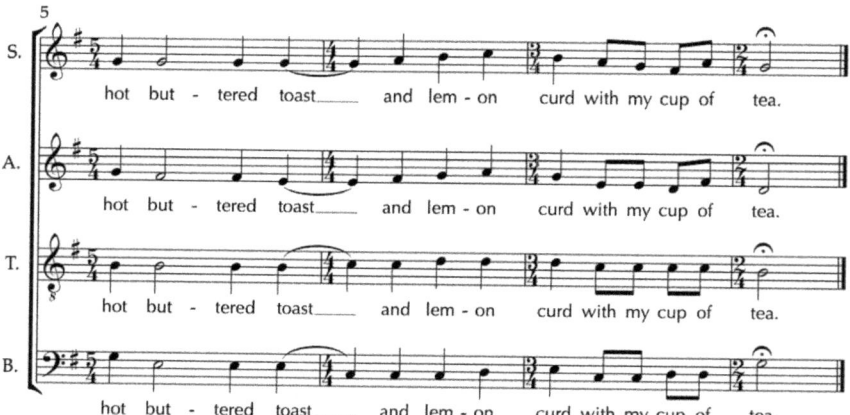

Exercise 1. Syllables

- Syllables, elision, phrasing, and blend all covered by this exercise
- Steady tempo required
- Consistent dynamic required.

Cut Glass

Exercise 2. More syllables

- Use the dynamics printed on the exercise
- Underline the choir's need for listening to each other, sounding the unpitched consonants, and supporting the pitched consonants and vowels with good breath support.

Spiritui Sancto
- syllable placing/listening

Exercise 3. More syllables and listening

- The rhythmically complicated entries will require significant discipline to sound the consonants, support the vowel production and phrase through the quavers or semiquavers to keep a consistent sound, which blends with the other parts effectively
- The exercise should be performed on one breath in cut (?) common time for added challenge!

These exercises are just a few examples of the types of exercises I have found useful when helping choirs to focus on delivering the most effective diction. There are many more exercises that can help in the same way. Feel free to use and/or adapt these exercises accordingly as you listen to the developmental changes that begin to affect your choir's overall sound.

Chapter 11: Listening to Create Vocal Colours

Conductors who work with the human voice are aware that the vocal mechanism can produce different vocal tones or colours, depending on how the different parts are manipulated in order to do so.

For the purposes of this discussion, I am referring to the biological mechanism for creating vocal sound as shown in the following diagram:

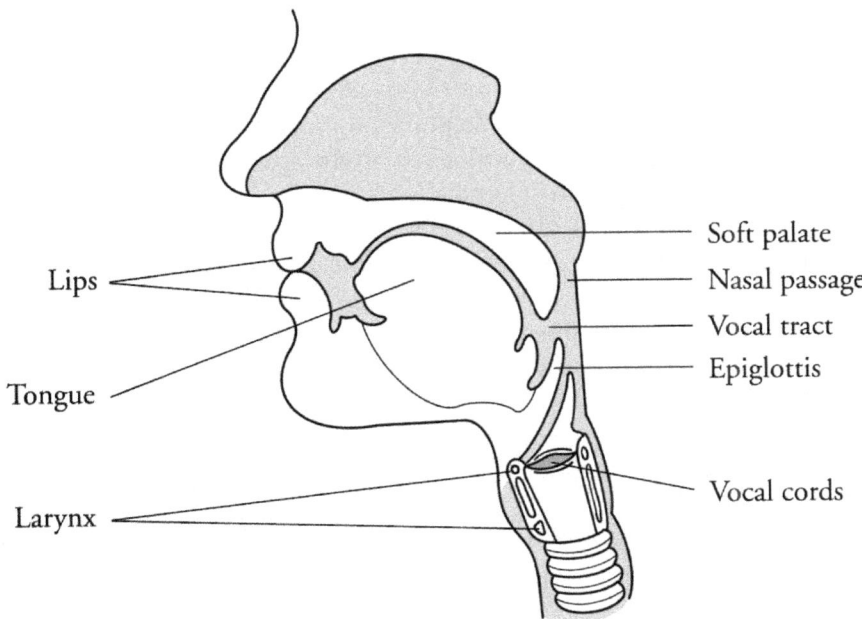

Light and Dark

In essence there are two basic types of vocal colour that all voice types can produce – that of a lighter sound and a darker sound. In this chapter I will explore the variety of ways in which the various muscles and organs of the upper vocal mechanism may be used to create a variety of lighter or darker sounds and how these might be rehearsed with a choir to achieve specific vocal effects. As we explore these, the reader may wish to return to the diagram above to confirm which areas are being discussed.

Sound is created by the vocal cords vibrating. When the sound passes through the vocal tract it is here that it can be manipulated. The vocal tract is the area that is the whole of the mouth plus the nasal cavity. No one vocal tract is the same as another – they are unique per our individual bodies so it is not unusual for male bodies to have smaller vocal tracts and female bodies to have larger vocal tracts, or *vice versa* but its size does have influence on the sound and colour that is generated - to the point that voices are recognised by the individual sounds the vocal tract can make: hence we can recognise one another's voices when we speak or sing. Larger vocal tracts often can create a darker vocal sound and smaller vocal tracts a lighter sound.

We can move the position of our vocal tracts to change the vocal colour we produce because the tract itself is conjoined and so has influence over several other 'moving parts', which in turn help change the tract itself. The parts we can move are the tongue, the larynx, the epiglottic funnel, the mouth, the palate (soft and hard sections) and the nasal cavity.

Just as good speakers learn to keep an even vocal tone through elocution coaching, good singers learn the same with their singing tone.

The Effect of the Moving Parts

Epiglottic funnel:

If you look in the mirror at the inside of your mouth and can see the back of the throat, you might be able to see the following:

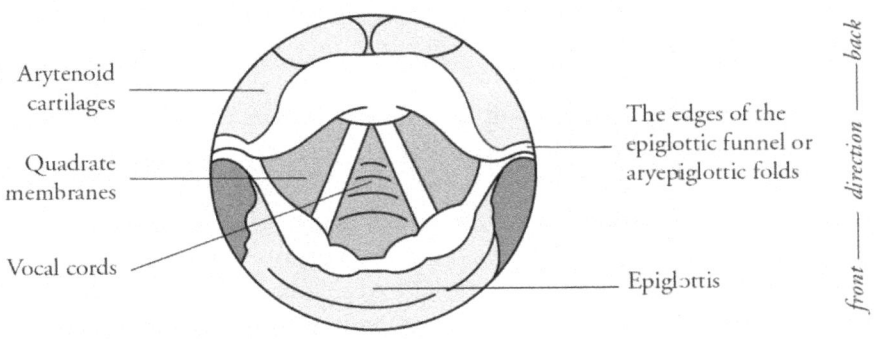

Epiglottic funnel seen from above

The more the arytenoid cartilages get closer to the lower part of epiglottis, the more twanged the sound will become.

Here you can see how the epiglottic funnel (E.F.) is created by the cartilages that hang down (a little bit like a pair of curtains), the quadratic membranes – which are above the vocal cords, the edges of the funnel on each side (the aryepiglottic folds) and the space down to the vocal cords themselves. The whole opening, overhung by the 'curtains' of the Arytenoid cartilages, is the epiglottal funnel, which we can manipulate through widening, broadening, flattening, or elongating. As we change the position, or shape of the opening of the funnel, we change the timbre of the sound we make when we sing.

This manipulation of the epiglottic funnel is sometimes referred to as 'vocal twang'.

The result of such manipulation of the epiglottic funnel is a vocal sound that is much sharper in tone which also increases in volume.

Twang

There are two types of vocal twang, but both should work in combination with the whole vocal and breathing mechanism. The two types are in combination with either a chest voice/natural twang or a more nasal sounding voice – a more emphatic twang. Some exercises appear in this chapter that may be worth trying out with your choir but here are some brief explanations and examples of how to create both twangs:

Natural Twang

As choral directors, we can help our singers obtain a better clarity and intensity of vocal sound by constructing vocal exercises that need the epiglottic funnel to be 'flattened' somewhat: imagine a sieve, if you like, which has a changeable setting for how large or small the holes for the sieve action are set – small holes create a more purer sieved bowl of flour than large holes which might let extraneous bits of hardened flour through. Vocally, we hope our singers will perform with as much clarity and purity of tone (smaller sieve holes) as possible and we can influence the tone our singers use by way of warm up exercises we then later refer to in our rehearsals of a piece of music.

Where the sides of the E.F. are flattened and widened as necessary during what we might describe as 'normal singing'. The E.F. will fluctuate in position in a way that allows singers to create well rounded or 'well placed' vowel sounds without totally impeding the airflow needed to create them. Natural twang is most helpful if the choir needs an impactful sound for a specific performance effect but adding this colour into general singing is encouraged as the use of it also relieves vocal tension created by over working some of the supporting musculature in the face and neck. Quick ways to create twang in your singers include asking them to make the following noises as part of a warmup:

- Quacking like a duck
- Cackling like a witch
- Making the 'nee naw' sound of an emergency vehicle
- Meowing like a cat

As choral leaders, the key to us using twang to enhance a particular passage is having spent time ourselves working out where and why it is of use. Using it for the sake of its use is not helpful to your choir but if it used to help the choir sustain tone and timbre through a particularly difficult (possibly high)interval with a vowel sound that lends itself to reasonable twang (aah, eh, ee) then it becomes an effective and vocally healthy tool.

Emphatic Twang

This is similar to the Natural Twang mentioned above except that the E.F. is very closed, creating a much more piercing vocal sound (imagine the vocal effect of a sudden cry or sob and its impact on your ears). As directors we can rehearse this kind of sound in isolation, much as mentioned previously but we might expect to use this technique at very specific or dramatic points in a passage of music or work. It is best rehearsed with a sound that is extreme – a sob, perhaps – and then worked into context within a sung phrase with your singers: demonstration of where exactly the emphatic twang is executed will be important in your rehearsal so that singers can hear it without getting bogged down in too much biology unnecessarily.

However, the E.F. is not the only part of the system that can have influence over a singer's sound:

The (soft) **Palate**, if raised, allows more air to flow through the E.F. and helps create a darker tone, whereas when it is lowered the tone becomes lighter.

The **Nasal Passages**, if closed, aid the creation of a darker tone but if opened help a lighter tone (*n.b.* This is in direct corelation with a more nasal twang – sounds nasal but isn't)

The position of the **Larynx** can also help change the tonal colour – a lowered larynx helps produce a darker sound and the raised larynx helps produce a lighter sound.

The use of the **Tongue** has an impact on the tone colour too – a tongue that is compressed helps create a darker tone and a broader, more relaxed tongue helps toward a lighter tone.

The **Mouth** also contributes to tonal colour: if the corners of the mouth are relaxed and in 'default' position, they can help produce a darker sound, whilst if we extend the corners of the mouth, this can help with creating a lighter sound.

On the extreme sides of the darkest and lightest tonal colours possible to create, we can draw up a prescriptive list of contributing moving parts that help in getting the colours we hope to achieve in a given passage of music. They are:

Creating the darkest tone:	**Creating the lightest tone:**
Relaxed corners of the mouth Compressing the tongue Lowering the larynx Singing with the Natural Twang Raising the soft palate Closing the nasal passages Singing with a more Emphatic Twang	Extending the corners of the mouth Broadening and flattening the tongue Raising the larynx Lowering the soft palate Opening the nasal passages Singing with a more Emphatic Twang

On examining the lists above it becomes clearer that these prescriptive elements can be rehearsed with a choir to create these different vocal colours.

What kinds of exercises might we run – either as part of a warmup, or, to underline a specific vocal need during a rehearsal of some music, to help us achieve the tonal colours we would like during a performance?

Vocal Colour Exercises

Here follows some example exercises which might help us achieve these different vocal colours. Singers should try these exercises within their own vocally comfortable octaves:

Vocal Colour Exercise 1

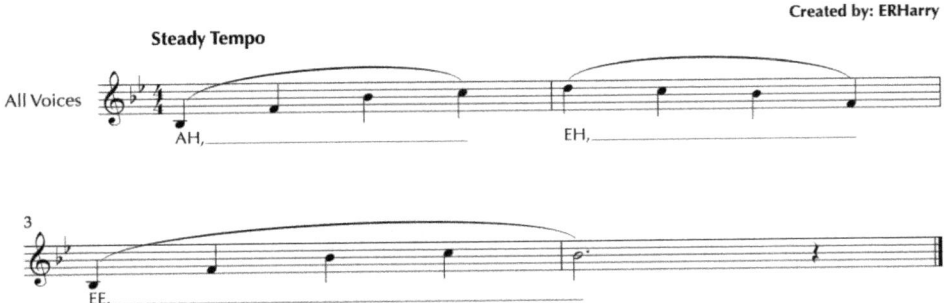

Vocal Colour Exercise 1 Suggestions

- Try this exercise with varying tongue position; sometimes flattened and broadened, sometimes lifted higher and ask the choir to listen to the different vocal colours that are made
- Try this exercise with the choir singing whilst fully smiling, just turning the corners of their mouth up as in the start of a smile and then whilst trying to push the corners of their mouth to each side, whilst again listening to the vocal colours produced. Then try adding some text from a piece of music that the choir might be familiar with or that they are currently working on

Vocal Colour Exercise 2

Created by: ERHarry

Vocal Colour Exercise 2 Suggestions

- Try asking the choir to sing this whilst they turn the corners of their mouths down whilst flaring their nostrils. This should make a rather 'haughty' (dark) vocal sound (this helps the choir lower their soft palate)
- Then try asking them to sing this exercise whilst making the vocal colour most closely associated to an over the top 'cackling old witch or wizard' – this helps the choir raise their soft palate
- Then ask them to try the exercise by switching between the two positions above per bar
- At the end, ask them to sing the exercise 'normally' and they (and you) should notice that their overall tone has a 'brighter' ring to it, as the natural twang is easier to create after moving the palate position

Vocal Colour Exercise 3

Created by: ERHarry

Vocal Colour Exercise 3 Suggestions

- First practice this singing 'normally' so the choir learns where the text underlay is placed correctly
- When the choir have learned it, ask the choir to sing it with a raised larynx (shortcut – ask the singers to start to yawn, as they do so their mouths open and the larynx raises, then ask them to stop the yawn but maintain the raised larynx position) and listen to how lighter their tone has become, ask them to listen for this too and explain that raising the larynx can help keep a more even tone in music that crosses the passaggio in their ranges
- Now try the exercise with a lowered larynx position (frowning will help with this) and listen to the darker tone created as the frowning also squeezes the epiglottic funnel to a more closed position. Singing with the larynx in this position may even impede on the quality of tone produced for the notes above the upper C.

Vocal Colour Exercise 4

Created by: ERHarry

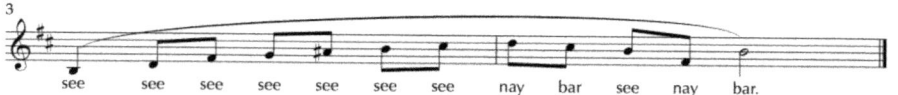

Vocal Colour Exercise 4 Suggestions

- Try asking the singers (once they have learned the notes and text underlay) to sing this whilst trying to close their nasal passages and notice the vocal colours that occur as the nasal passages are closed and then open somewhat when the singers need to take a breath
- Try asking the singers to practice their vocal 'sob' in this exercise and listen to the impact of the more emphatic twang on their voices

Headline Advice for Vocal Colour:

- Slip these exercises into warm up activities at the start of the rehearsal and refer to them when you are looking for a certain vocal colour or effect in a particular passage of music, during the main rehearsal
- Vocal colour exercises can be highly amusing for the choir so enjoy it, let them laugh at you should you demonstrate the colours you are looking for and then let them laugh with each other as they all attempt it
- Don't forget that the basis of all achievable vocal colour is knowing the score and what you'd like to achieve with it – and then applying either a dark tone or light tone plan for your vocal colour exercises

Chapter 12: Vocal Health & Development: Listening for Vocal Changes

Conductors may find themselves in the position of being approached by members of their choirs, seeking advice on vocal health matters. As the designated director of a singing ensemble, singers may naturally choose to approach the leader for advice in this area. Good choral directors will be aware of vocal ergonomics as part of their approach to the musical leadership of any ensemble and should be prepared to listen, assess and then, if confident and comfortable, offer some basic advice or be able to refer singers to someone professionally able to help.

This chapter aims to discuss, in broad terms only, some of the more common vocal ailments and other vocal developments that might become a topic of conversation with singers seeking advice in a choral setting.

General Overuse of the Voice

In a recent survey of choral singers in Finland[3], 21% of those surveyed registered a general vocal complaint. Developing the following vocal complaints is common if the voice is overused regularly:

- Vocal dryness
- Hoarseness
- Phonasthenia (vocal fatigue)
- Tightness in the throat
- Reduced pitch range
- Throat pain
- Voice breaks

---

[3] Ravall, Sofie: Logopedics, Master's Thesis (2015) Åbo Akademi University, Finland

- Difficulty being heard
- Constant need to clear the throat

Choral leaders may become aware of their singers showing some of these symptoms, either through observation during a rehearsal or by the singer reporting it to the leader and possibly requesting advice, as mentioned earlier. Monitoring the general overuse of voices is something that can easily be achieved in rehearsals by combining listening with observation of those singing. It should be noted that the above listed symptoms are also present when the vocal cords have become swollen or inflamed and can be accompanied by a mild fever.

It should also be noted that prolonged inactivity as a singer (due to reasons such as illness, pandemic isolation etc.) may well incur some of the symptoms listed above. Singers should be encouraged not to over sing but to relax and sing as they are able, without 'forcing' a vocal sound. They should also be encouraged to drink plenty of water some hours before a rehearsal to ensure that they are well hydrated before singing. When experiencing an ailment such as those listed above, singers may need to be patient, as the vocal mechanisms are muscles that need regular exercise to be in the best condition. Like all exercise regimes, their vocal mechanisms may need to be 'built up again' following prolonged absence. Singers should be patient, and conductors should be empathetic, understanding and encouraging

The Vocal Cords

The vocal cords (or vocal folds) are two membrane-like bands of tissue that are housed in the larynx.

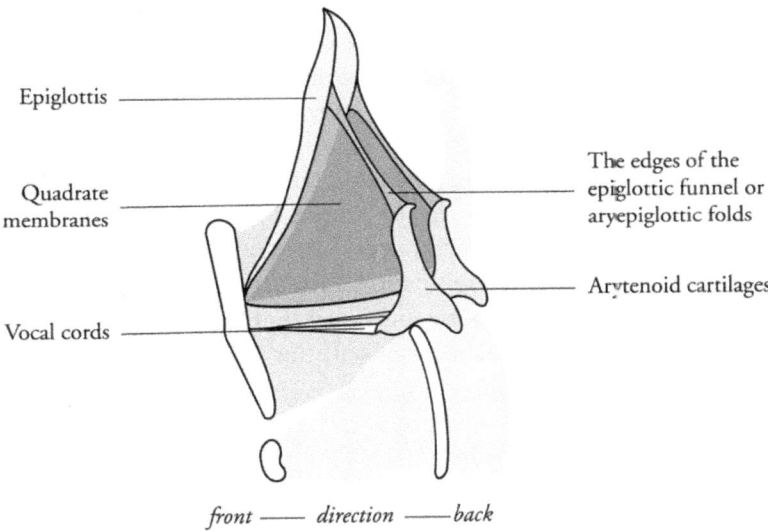

Epiglottic funnel seen from the side

- Epiglottis
- Quadrate membranes
- Vocal cords
- The edges of the epiglottic funnel or aryepiglottic folds
- Arytenoid cartilages

front —— direction ——back

The two membranes vibrate whilst air is pushed through them via the lungs to create the tone of the voice.

Vocal Cord Disorders

Laryngitis – where the vocal cords are inflamed. The symptoms produced are a raspy vocal tone or hoarseness to the point of loss of the speaking voice. The back of the throat may feel dry and sore.

Vocal Nodules – noncancerous lumps or callouses on the vocal cords caused by misuse (or abuse) of the voice. Professional singers may encounter this problem due to the regular intense use of their voices. They often grow in pairs and often form on the part of the vocal cords that are under most pressure when the cords come together and vibrate. Symptoms are hoarseness, lower sounding and/or breathy tone.

Vocal Polyps – noncancerous growth. Similar in nature to a blister. Blood can be included in the blister, which eventually clears to form a transparent or milky white blister. As in nodules, polyps cause the voice to have symptoms of hoarseness and a lower sounding and/or breathy tone.

Vocal Cord Paralysis – this is when one or both cords do not open or close properly. If one cord is weak or non-moving, the voice sounds weak and food or drink may enter the trachea and lungs, which in turn causes trouble swallowing, choking and/or coughing when eating. If both cords are paralysed the person can have difficulty breathing. Common causes of vocal cord paralysis include injuries to the head, neck or chest, stroke, issues during surgical procedures, viral infections, tumours, lung cancer, thyroid cancer, some neurological disorders such as Multiple Sclerosis and Parkinson's Disease. Treatments for this condition may include surgery and vocal therapy though there is evidence that sufferers can recover without medical intervention.

Spasmodic Dysphonia – where a nerve problem causes the vocal cords to spasm spontaneously.

Treatment for any of the above can depend on your age and overall health. Examples of treatment can include:

- Stopping singing or the behaviour that is deduced as the aggravating factor
- Total vocal rest
- Referral to a consultant speech therapist or vocal masseur
- Medical intervention
- Surgery to remove callouses, growths or polyps

Some possible causes of vocal injury are:

- Smoking
- Uncontrolled or untreated acid reflux
- Singing too loudly
- Singing with poor vocal technique

- Forcing the voice whilst suffering with a cold or a bronchial infection (e.g., bronchitis)

The key points to remember are:

- Any vocal cord disorder is likely to affect both your singing and speech voices
- Vocal cord disorders are commonly caused by misuse of the voice
- Symptoms can include raspy voice, hoarseness, difficulty swallowing, coughing, or choking when eating
- Vocal cord disorders are preventable by changing vocal behaviour
- Any singer who complains of the general symptoms of hoarseness, raspy tone, coughing, or trouble swallowing for over 2 weeks should see their GP as soon as possible.

Conductors should take care to ensure that their direction does not ask for their singers to overuse nor misuse their voices. It is suggested that choral conductors ensure their knowledge of vocal pedagogy and anatomy is up to date and is 'fed into' regular rehearsals. There is a growing set of resources on vocal health in many countries and online: support and training should be sought, to enable conductors to direct with the vocal health of their singers in mind, in all rehearsals. If this is not possible, conductors are encouraged to approach vocal coaches to help support their ensemble's vocal health during rehearsals.

Changing Voices - Cambiata

A cambiata choir is a choir for boys at the adolescent stage, whose voices are in the process of changing. This important type of choir exists to encourage boys to keep singing as they progress through the stages of vocal development associated with their developing maturity.

Conductors who work with choirs of this nature will always be listening to how its member's voices are changing and progressing. They may work with choral repertoire written especially for voices at this stage and it is worth understanding the process the male voice undergoes as it matures.

When boys begin to grow due to the onset of adolescence, facial bones, sinus cavities, the nose and the back of the throat, grow. So, the larynx and vocal cords grow significantly thicker and longer too, producing more space in the head for the voice to resonate and causing the pitch of the voice to deepen. This vocal development can be accompanied by a period of vocal unsteadiness where the pitch of the speaking and/or singing voice sharply alternates between the previously higher pitch and the now more prevalent deeper pitch as the vocal cords tighten and relax as they develop. Boys sometimes have an initial struggle with singing pitches consistently through this process but if they keep their voice training consistent throughout their vocal development they will learn how to manage their newly developed young adult vocal mechanisms.

Conductors of cambiata choirs or of youth choirs with mixed ages memberships, should be sensitive toward these changes as boys may be easily embarrassed by their vocal unsteadiness. Every encouragement will be needed to keep them singing and listening carefully to spot vocal changes and unsteadiness will be key to supporting those singers who are going through the process.

More Serious Medical Issues

Vocal Cord Lesions (cancerous) and laryngeal cancer can show itself in the following symptoms:

- A change in the timbre of the voice (e.g., Hoarseness)
- A swelling or lump in the neck
- Long lasting coughing or breathlessness
- Constant sore throat and/or earache
- Pain when swallowing or difficulty swallowing
- A wheezing sound when breathing in and out
- Difficulty breathing

You will note that some of these symptoms overlap with those mentioned earlier in the chapter and so referral to a GP should always be at the forefront of a conversation with a singer who presents with any symptoms in these lists.

Ageing

Ageing is a process we all go through and it can affect singers in a number of ways. Amateur choir memberships often include those who have decided to take up choral singing as they wind down their working career or retire and so managing and supporting ageing voices is an important aspect of The Listening Conductor's role.

As the period of 'middle age' begins to come to an end it is not uncommon for all genders to notice a lowering of vocal pitch. Quite naturally, the larynx drops position in our post middle age years, which creates a bigger distance from the vocal cords to the mouth (or vocal tract). This increase in the length of the vocal tract changes its influence on vocal resonance and the outworking of this are enhanced lower vocal frequencies – so the voice sounds lower.

Female Menopause

At the end of 'middle age', hormonal changes related to menopause change the vocal cords; they become stiffer and slightly thickened or swollen. The mucus-producing glands that help to lubricate them reduce in number, which causes dryness. These changes significantly impact on the pitch by lowering it and creating a breathier or rougher sound tone to the vocal quality.

Male changes post middle age

Men are more likely to have a higher vocal range in this part of their lives; the vocal folds tend to become thinner and stiffer, thus creating a thinner vocal but higher vocal pitch. Sometimes the inner 'lip' of the cords lose their ability to meet in the middle, resulting in a breathier tone, in the higher register particularly. This condition – Presbylarynx - occurs mostly in men of very advanced years but can also occur in elderly women.

All genders must accept that the laryngeal cartilages will calcify and that the cricoarytenoid joints (which are linked to the opening and closing of the vocal cords) become stiffer, with ageing. Closing the vocal folds becomes more difficult and the vocal tone becomes steadily breathier, whilst higher notes may not sound, or 'cut out'.

These changes are usually gradual however evidence is beginning to emerge from continuing research that the recent global COVID-19 pandemic lockdowns have either exacerbated or accelerated these conditions in older singers who were unable to sing for close to 2 years, as a result.

Advice to Ageing Singers

If conductors are approached by older singers seeking support and guidance around their continued singing, this is wholly positive. The primary symptom that emerges from ageing singers is not any of the above but is a loss of confidence in their voices and their ability to contribute to the functioning of a singing ensemble or choir, effectively. This, in turn, leads to self-questioning as to their individual worth to the whole group in which they sing. Here are some points of advice to consider offering to older singers with these concerns:

- Suggest doing a vocal warm up every day, regardless of whether there is any singing activity happening
- Keeping singing is the best way to retain strength and energy in the muscles needed to be able to sing, so giving up should only be a last resort
- Regular exercise of a general nature, like walking, is important to keep the body fit and healthy. Also exercise like Yoga and/or Pilates
- A healthy and varied diet will also contribute to maintaining a healthy body (including the vocal mechanisms)
- Keep well hydrated before, during, after rehearsals
- Give up smoking
- Keep alcohol intake to a minimum – alcohol is known to contribute to Acid Reflux, as well as to be irritating to the vocal cords
- Keep mentally active – crosswords, puzzles, online games (that don't include betting)
- Have your hearing checked regularly
- Explain to your ageing singer that their contribution is needed now as much as ever and that their presence and efforts are really appreciated by the conductor and any managing board or committee

A Note on Vocal Warmups

Warm up exercises are an important start to any rehearsal. They:

- Re-engage or remind singers of the various parts of the vocal mechanism
- Help rehearse those muscles that contribute to a healthy singing tone
- Help focus the rehearsal
- Help re-initiate the relationship and teamwork ethic between leader and singers

- Help singers practice placing solid consonant and vowel shapes and sounds within specially designed, isolated vocal exercises - out of context of the music being rehearsed

Warmups are a good opportunity for a choral leader to listen to the singers, to work on general choral techniques such as blend, diction, and elision and also to possibly identify voices that may not be fully healthy and to potentially diagnose the reason why.

That is not to suggest that leaders should then approach individual singers with possible diagnoses. They should not. If a vocal issue is obvious to many in the room there might be a cause to take the lead on its discussion but otherwise leaders should wait to be approached, keeping a personal note on what might have been heard.

It is important to note that warmups do have vocal health benefits: they are a good opportunity to briefly focus in on one or more specific exercise that aids singers to re-engage with their vocal mechanisms, perhaps with an explanatory reminder of why certain exercises are helpful to singers in a choir. Warmups are always more effective if they are accompanied by very brief explanations of why they exist and how they help singers prepare for a rehearsal. Well planned warmups will include:

- palate placement exercises
- abdominal muscle support exercises
- singing through the comfortable vocal ranges
- sirening
- sighing, yawning
- lip and tongue trills
- massages of the facial and cranio-facial muscles (to help release tension)
- humming (good for working the vocal cords without exertion)
- 'tongue twisters' (which help with focus, as well as good diction)
- energy and fun

For more information on how to help your choir with excellent warm-ups, *How to Make Your Choir Sound Awesome* by Lucy Hollins and Suzzie Vango is an invaluable resource.

Headline Advice for Vocal Ailments:

- Any symptoms that have shown for 2 weeks or more should be checked by a GP
- Listen, empathise but do not try to diagnose
- Build healthy warm-up exercises into your regime
- Observe your singers and coach them into singing healthily if you spot overuse or misuse of the voice
- Developing male voices should expect to be unsteady
- Ageing voices should be patient and work on singing every day

Chapter 13: Listening to Feedback

Being part of a group of people, however small or large, means that not everyone will share the same opinion. Most of the time our opinions can and should be put aside to create the best standard of music but sometimes a person can become indelibly distracted by something that occurs during a rehearsal, or, over a specific choice of music programming.. Here are some thoughts a singing choir member might become preoccupied with:

- The clothes the conductor is wearing or a 'wardrobe malfunction'
- Warm-up exercises seem pointless
- Rehearsing the same piece for the umpteenth time
- Difficulty in hearing what the conductor is saying because they are not 'speaking up' enough
- Incorrect or varying pronunciation of text and/or interpretation of rhythm
- The tempo is too slow or too fast for the singer's liking
- The singer doesn't agree with the beating pattern of the conductor
- Why are we singing this music? Who chose it?

One of the aspects of conducting or singing in a choir that is rarely discussed is that there are times when we receive feedback. At some point, we all must face the fact that singing together or conducting a group of singers puts us in the position of naturally inviting (albeit subconsciously sometimes) feedback on what we are doing.

Listening to Feedback: Singer to Singer

All sorts of people join a choir: some are sensitive, others are insensitive; some are well mannered and wouldn't dream of upsetting another singer on purpose, whilst others are just plain rude. The saying 'all life is here' absolutely describes each voice section of a choir — amateur or professional.

(new para) Our voices are a part of our bodies and singers on joining a choir are willing to 'share' their singing voice with others who will hear them. Some singers have years of singing experience and some may have little or no experience. There are times when singers feel that it is acceptable to make a comment, positive or negative, on the voices they hear around them. How that comment is received and interpreted can vary; some singers may be offended and hurt, others dismiss it or may be pleased to listen to feedback from peers and colleagues in their own section. Singers must develop their own personal strategies for dealing with both positive and negative or unwanted feedback. If an individual in a voice section becomes a 'regular target' of negative feedback from one or more persons in a voice section, then a bystander or the person receiving the feedback should contact a voice section representative or a member of the leadership group of the choir for support and guidance. Conductors can offer vocal coaching and advice if necessary to either affirm or dismiss any feedback, however, conductors should not involve themselves with the management of the situation any further than this. I have conducted choirs where several members stayed away from rehearsals because of an individual making negative comments. This is not healthy or helpful to the development of a voice section and should be dealt with by those elected to do so.

Listening to Feedback:
Singer to Conductor – Six Strategies for Listening and Responding

Conductors must accept that in choral preparing, they alone are leading. With that leadership comes the responsibility of having to prepare for the rehearsal, plan for areas of improvement and ensure that the aims and objectives for each session are achieved. If those targets are not met, conductors need to adjust the rehearsal schedule, which is the framework for preparing any performance. In addition, conductors put themselves in the somewhat vulnerable position of receiving direct feedback in front of the group at any time. They must accept that this may happen and, therefore, learn strategies that help them respond appropriately to the feedback they receive.

Here follows a set of six strategies for possible adopting or adapting, as required:

Strategy 1: No-open-feedback policy

It is possible to work with choirs on having a no-open-feedback policy. This means that feedback is collected either in written form and then sent to the conductor for consideration or is fed back to the conductor face-to-face following a rehearsal, giving the conductor time to respond appropriately in the next session or via email in between sessions.

Strategy 2: "Thank you, I'll answer at the end."

Feedback is received openly during the rehearsal, but the response is made at an appropriate later juncture, so as not to disrupt the pace of the rehearsal so much.

Strategy 3: "That's a good question, thank you for asking it, here's the answer…"

Feedback is received and the answer given immediately; the answer is reiterated and underlined metaphorically, so everyone can hear it and make a note for themselves.

Strategy 4: 'I'm sorry you disagree; I will take some time to think about that and then come back to you if I want to change what I'm doing but thanks for the input.'

Give yourself time to think about whether the input should be considered or not. It also is a polite response that acknowledges the feedback listened to, so the person suggesting does not feel dismissed or embarrassed.

Strategy 5: 'Thank you for the suggestion but no. I have made clear what I'd like to happen at that point and I'd like to keep to that for now.'

This is polite but firm and communicates a definite negative response to the input offered. Best done with an acknowledging smile to the person who offered the input.

Strategy 6: 'I think you'll find that that is exactly what I said a few minutes ago to the basses and then asked everyone to do the same but you might not have heard it?'

It is possible, nay probable, that someone might ask a question that has been answered shortly before. This can happen for several reasons, but let's assume it is because either that person was not listening or simply didn't hear your direction when it was given. This response points that out but also helps the person asking not to feel embarrassed by providing a 'get-out clause' at the end!

It is worth noting that good direction may inspire those in a choir to want to respond, which can be both helpful and constructive. Inappropriately timed feedback can also be both unhelpful and disruptive and needs careful management during a rehearsal.

Groundswell: Listening to Strong Opinions

Opinions held by individuals are often shared for validation purposes. For example, if someone feels aggrieved, they may want to know if others agree with their feelings. It is possible that those with whom this opinion is shared, will go on to share it with others. So, a 'groundswell' of opinion may start to bubble away amongst members of a choir. As a conductor or singer, you may become aware of groundswell brewing in the background — positive or negative. However, it is best not to get involved in groundswell, but remain willing to offer your opinion if asked for, and if it will help.

I once worked with a choir that stayed silent on a subject or a piece of music if they approved of its inclusion. If there was feedback and 'general chatter', it was because they disapproved! These behavioural patterns are worth observing, analysing and understanding as they will help both a singer and a conductor come to understand the choir they direct much better. But how do we manage groundswell or growing opinion?

Strategy 1: Positive groundswell

If the opinion is a positive one, listen as to why, the insight may help you with other decisions later.

Strategy 2: Negative groundswell built on incorrect information or assumption

Acknowledge to yourself that the opinion exists but choose not to become involved. Should someone approach you for your opinion of this, give one and see if that answer is fed back to the 'opinion leaders' and the groundswell fades away. If not, do not be afraid to repeat your response as part of your rehearsal; build it into your feedback to the choir as you rehearse but do not mention the reason why you are highlighting it. Singers should always direct those leading a growing groundswell of opinion to someone managing the choir — and not to the conductor. The aim is to abate the groundswell by having it reported so that something can be done about it.

Strategy 3: Negative groundswell on the direction the choir is taking or the music it is performing

'It is not possible to please everyone' was one of the things a long-serving chairperson of a managing committee of a choir wisely pointed out to me, early on in my professional career. They were right, of course. Whatever decisions are made, whether it concerns the music that is programmed, which venue hosts a concert, or what type of clothes are worn — not everyone will be happy. Most singers join a choir because they want to be a part of it, perform with others, contribute to it and whether they admit it not, have a personal passion for choral singing and choral music. It should be the same for conductors of choral music too. That personal passion translates to much time thinking and reflecting on how the choir is doing — what could be improved and what is going well. If there is a particular issue with how the choir is developing or the music it is rehearsing and performing, it is not uncommon for passionate feelings to spill over into groundswell of opinion. Singers should be prepared to report their feelings to the appropriate person and see what happens as a result. If nothing happens, this must be accepted; harbouring ill-will will develop into deeper ill-feeling and will result in their membership of the choir becoming a negative experience. Formally giving their opinion must also come with the psychological action of 'letting it go' —for the sake of others around them and for their own wellbeing. It is always worth reminding ourselves why we joined the choir in the first place. For singing and for enjoyment!

If you are a conductor, you should expect periods where the choir lets you know that it's not happy with some things or very happy with others. All things being equal, it is worth treating all feedback concerning the choir's development or music programming in the same, balanced way by analysing why the feedback has been given. Music choices are often temporary — they may last up to a concert and then disappear. If you direct a single-sex choir, it is possible that the music programming will remain the same for a period but singing music we don't like doesn't have to stop us learning how to sing, phrase, breathe and improve musically. A choir should always be developing its sound, blend, *raison d'etre*. However, a conductor may want to develop a choir in ways that the members feel is not appropriate —too 'modern' or different, or just not in keeping with the choirs' wishes. The way to avoid this is through transparency within the management structure of the choir and a solid development plan agreed between all parties. The development plan should be in place in the early stages of a conductor working with a choir, so that there are no surprises. It might even be worth sharing this with the choir themselves.

Managing the Management:
Listening to Your Contractors

Those of us who work with choirs fall into one of the following categories:

- Contract of employment by Church diocese
- Contract of employment to established branded choir(s) and orchestra or another organisation (artist contract)
- Contracted for services (freelance)
- Conducting is an unmentioned part of the contract of employment (e.g., education)

- Unpaid volunteer with no contract.

Whichever category we fit into, we will have to navigate many things when leading a choir, the most obvious of which is listening to those who oversee our work in one capacity or another. This can present difficulties if those overseeing our work have not studied music and have little management or human resource experience. It is important that conductors retain a sense of professionalism throughout all processes – whether that's working for a professional arts organisation, community-based choir, or any other organisation. Conductors must learn to listen and then be sure they understand what it is that is being communicated to them by reflecting what they think is being said back to those who are managing them - and managing the relationship between them and the choir for affirmation. Listening is important when talking with those who oversee our contractual obligations and conductors should work toward a trusted relationship with their contractors. Listening and responding positively, regardless of the conversation is one way to build up this relationship. There are times when responding positively to certain situations may prove incredibly challenging. However, rather than responding negatively, make a note of the challenging thing that is being asked of you and offer to provide a response after you have had time to think about it. In the meantime, do think and reflect on it, talk it through with a trusted friend or find a mentor or colleague to talk with. Conductors should be supportive of one another, despite the competitive industry in which we work. Responding to your overseeing manager in this way shows transparency and is itself a positive response, even if the final answer is not.

Listening to Working Groups

Some choirs have a committee structure that might include more than one working group to discuss initiatives or developments. Some of the internal structures of how and when the groups operate may be traditional or modern, may have been in place for many years, or are recent. It can be overwhelming for a conductor to realise that there are many people involved in the decision-making process — even down to the choice of music for the concerts at Christmas, Easter, and the

Summer. Inexperienced conductors may struggle with being 'the only musically qualified person in the room', but for most people, choral music is a real passion, meaning even the most inexperienced members may want to have input into planning and development.

When working with a choir that has a working group or committee, it is fundamental to remember that choirs have their own histories, funny stories, memorable moments and sense of community. Those members who are involved with the machinations of making the choir 'work' are very often volunteers who are giving their time for free. As conductors we need to remember that the reason we can meet with members to discuss ideas, innovations and developments, is because of the willingness of volunteers. Professional choirs may have slightly different set-ups but somewhere along the line, someone is going to be giving up their time. Listening to the thoughts, memories, ideas, advice, and considerations of the members of such groups is important. Conductors need to support the decision-making of such groups with wise and considered musical — or otherwise — counsel.

Having said this, decisions do have to be made and sometimes the experiences and knowledge of a musical director or accompanist can directly influence the outcomes of planning decisions or ideas for new projects. If a conductor feels that decisions made by a working group compromise their own working methods, beliefs or understanding of the working relationship, the conductor must raise this with someone on a management group or committee, rather than accept being over-ruled or asked to do something that they do not agree with. It is important that a conductor is listened to as much as anyone else working for the good of the choir.

Chapter 14: Criticism

Personal or private feedback: unwanted advice

There is a common saying that 'unwanted advice is criticism' and both conductors and singers are exposed to regular 'unwanted advice'. It is common because singing and leading a choir are 'public' activities. Activities where others can watch and listen to what we do. By performing these activities in public, we naturally invite responses; those responses generally fall into these categories: comment, opinion, or criticism.

In a rehearsal or following a public performance, we naturally respond to the reactions of others by quickly deciding if the communication prompted by our performance or leadership falls into one of those three categories. Then, when we have decided for ourselves which category the proffered reaction falls into, we respond or react accordingly. Looking at these categories more closely, they are:

- **Comment**. Simply a descriptive reaction to what has been said or sung, possible affirming or confirming the meaning
- **Opinion**. A subjective response invoked by something that is performed or directed. "I agree because…" or "I disagree because…", "I like that idea of…", "I don't think you've made this clear enough…"
- **Criticism**. "Why did you say that? It's not true!", "Are you always going to be so critical of the sopranos?" "You've got that German pronunciation wrong.".

Note the difference, magnified here, between opinion and criticism: opinions start with 'I' and criticism starts with 'You'.

In my time as a singer and conductor I have found myself on the receiving end of some truly remarkable 'unwanted advice' and I know I am far from alone. At times, it has been difficult to work out how to respond in as professional manner as possible. During my artistic endeavours, I have been grateful for the support and listening ears of supporters, friends and family who have always been willing to help me 'unburden' myself should the (often) intense 'unwanted advice' prove to be affecting me personally.

Perhaps the first, obvious thing to reiterate here is that singers and conductors are human. They can be built up by positivity and hurt by negativity: the only difference is that those who perform art in public can be looked upon as rather infallible or 'untouchable by comment'. Infallible we are not!

Listening to criticism can be difficult as it inevitably contains a degree of 'personal' about it, regardless of whether someone who is criticising begins the conversation with 'please don't take this personally but….' — or not.

Understanding where 'unwanted advice' comes from, helps to take some of the 'sting' out of it and as singers and conductors develop their careers, they are often left to discover the roots of — let's call it what it is — criticism, for themselves.

Before we look at ways of managing criticism, it is worth noting that all good artists make their craft look easy to the unknowing, critical observer.

Listening to Criticism: A Root Map

Experience has taught me that criticism can be broken down into certain categories. Here are the 'roots of criticism' to bear in mind when you are navigating your way to an appropriate response:

Being helpful. Sometimes people criticise because they are genuinely trying to be helpful and want to see you get better at what you do; they support and want to encourage you. This then leads to them wanting to inspire you to keep going and so they want you to hear their critical thoughts. The root of this is genuine support though it is not always easy to identify, initially.

Inspiration. At times, we can hit upon a directional point or sing something in a particular way that has an impact on others. They might suddenly realise that your point or performance would benefit from something they have learned, which you should consider. It can be offered as something you 'missed' or "what you could have said was…" or "you should have sung it this way because…"

Human connection. There are times when singers or directors can attract connections from those who are listening and responding to them. Sometimes we can be offered 'unasked for advice' by means of starting up a conversation and being friendly. 'Hello, just wondered if you had thought about…'. but the conversation has actually been started because the initiating person has been personally inspired by a style of leadership that has sparked a latent attraction of one type or another, in them.

Wanting to be needed. Sometimes singers or conductors can be offered 'unasked-for advice' by people who want to be seen as having an equal or greater understanding of a subject area than another singer or conductor. Be wary in this situation, as the person offering the 'advice' has a motivation that is rooted in themselves - and not the benefit of the group as a whole. "I know you said we should do it this way and I don't disagree, but I actually think we should…"

Feeling sorry for you. Singers and conductors are versed in connecting with their audiences on an emotional level. Singers may perform to recreate an operatic scene or the meaning of the text of a song; conductors may want to interpolate the dynamic markings in a score and align them with certain emotional states or dramatic meanings and, as a result, solicit a (possibly incorrect) emotionally supportive response. "I really felt for you when you were asking us to sing at *piano* for that bit. I'm sure we can do it properly for you, I'm sure we can. Why don't you ask us to…?"

Being narcissistic. This is the type of person who always wants us to know that they know more than everyone else. Their *modus operandi* is that of 'lecturing' on what the best way forward is for every decision — musical direction or performance interpretation. Long-winded diatribes put forward as 'a word to the wise', 'unwanted advice' encased in long descriptions of how they have seen it all and done it all and know the answers. As you see, the 'advice' is essentially an opportunity to talk about themselves, regardless of whether it is appropriate to the situation or not. "Well…when I did it, I did it this way because that's better than…"

Being dominant. Sometimes, persistent 'unwanted advice' is because the person providing it feels threatened by your knowledge, leadership style or performance skills. To address the perceived imbalance, they ascertain a dominant position: "I don't think you should do it that way, it won't work. Do it this way, I have and it works."

Being judgmental. Receiving 'unwanted advice' can have the hidden agenda of the person wanting to change the way you do things, so that they can then report to others that they have been 'influential' in changing how you work. This comes from judging what you do and judging it to be 'under par'. When we lead or perform, we put ourselves in an 'instant judgement line'. It's how we respond to being judged that is important. Sometimes those judging us can make valid points that we should act upon, other times not. Decide carefully how to respond.

Creating conflict. Sadly, there are people who enjoy being amidst conflict. Those people criticise for the sake of being critical, they like to stir things up and create a wider response other than just with us as leaders or singers. It is good to identify this type of person as soon as possible so that if criticism comes, we can understand the root cause and deal with it appropriately (by finding a calming response, not a response that will cause or exacerbate conflict or tension)

Self-Preservation whilst Listening

As performers, we can be affected by criticism, sometimes with good reason and at other times, unduly. There are occasions when, if we are working as full-time artists conducting or singing, the criticism can be both intense and constant. Or it can ebb and flow. Those criticising deliver their words of 'unasked for advice' without necessarily thinking of how those words might affect the person listening to them. However, as a performer, you should respond in a professional manner, despite how you might feel. This means that you might have little opportunity to express your true and honest feelings. You'll be receiving criticism but cannot be critical in return — a one-way conversation and one we should learn to manage effectively.

Self-preservation is a skill gained with experience. Performers learn to build an invisible barrier between themselves and those who are seeking to give 'unasked-for advice'. Should the 'arrows of criticism' penetrate that barrier and hit the soul, they won't stay there for long. Performers must be able to distance themselves from what is being discussed, try to see the subject discussed through other persons' eyes and be able to reflect on it objectively. That way performers protect themselves from potential emotional damage.

Handling Criticism the Right Way

There are many ways to handle criticism. Life-coaches, management training or friends and family will provide you with plenty of 'asked-for advice' in this arena. Here are some of the hints and tips picked up along the way:

- Listen first
- Reflect what you think you've heard back, using different words, to test your understanding of the critical comment
- Take time to reflect on whether the criticism is called for or not
- If not, respond to the criticism by thanking the provider and then explain why you will not be responding with any changes
- If the criticism is called for, thank the person for their comment and let them know how you will be responding
- If the criticism is personal, very unfair or damaging, ask the provider to repeat their critical comment in front of the chair of the main management committee or another higher representative from within the organisation, so it can be discussed properly and do not allow yourself to be alone with that individual in future if you think the criticism will remain
- Narcissistic criticisers should not be encouraged but if you find yourself having to listen to one, smile nicely, ignore what they say but make a note of it
- Conflict criticisers should be tolerated but expect to have to find ways to dampen their criticism

- Dominant criticisers find it difficult if you do not give a 'straight answer' to their criticism; "Oh right…we'll have to see about that…" let's them know that they have made their point, although they are now unsure if that point is being taken seriously.

It is important that musicians who lead choirs create for themselves a support mechanism made up of trusted friends, family, colleagues, and mentors. Conductors have a 'lonely' job in the judgement 'firing line'. The benefits for people's mental and physical wellbeing when taking part in music-making activities are now widely acknowledged. Therefore, it is important that those leading in these activities are supported as much as possible.

Whilst this chapter on 'criticism' may have made difficult reading for some, we must remember that criticism is almost always balanced out by those members of our choirs who are encouraging, mete out kind words, respond positively to direction and empathise with those leading in making music with the human voice.

Listening to Audience Feedback

Depending on the organisation you work for, there may be an opportunity to collect feedback from the audiences at your performances. On the other hand, you may sing with or lead a choir that has no mechanism at all for input from those who listen to you.

Collecting audience feedback can be difficult: when do you do it? Does the audience fill in a survey whilst at your performance? Do members of the choir go and 'meet and greet' audience members to ask them more informally what they thought of the performance? Is there an online form which audience members can fill in? Is there an online forum attached to your choir website where audience members are invited to leave feedback?

Whichever way it's done, audience feedback will likely be subjective in nature, boiling down to whether they like the music or not. In my experience, audience members do not wish to offend anyone by appearing to be overly critical, unless they themselves are either a choral singer or a musician of some kind. Therefore, the best kind of audience feedback is anonymous and possibly written sometime after the event, so that the listener has had time to form an objective opinion on what they have heard. Others argue that collecting feedback immediately after the event — whilst still at the venue — means that audience members are more honest about their first impressions.

It is, however, an important aspect of listening. The audience members who attend our performances are there for a reason and it is always worth finding out what the audience thinks of the performance they (may) have paid to attend. Our audiences might be paying for a ticket and it's always good to know if they feel they have had 'value for money'.

It is possible that an audience member might be inspired to share an idea they have had whilst listening to you sing or watch you conduct. It's always worth knowing if audience members pick up on things that 'weren't quite right' or things that went well. What impression has the singing left, or the presentation of the choir, the choice of music, the type of venue being performed in, the balance of sound, the choir's interaction with the conductor, whether the words could be heard clearly and the overall discipline of the choir as it performs. Feedback on all these elements can inspire us to proudly pat ourselves on the back or address things that 'didn't quite work'.

The good thing about collecting audience feedback, listening to it, and acting upon it if deemed necessary, is that that feedback is more likely to be genuine than not and so it does provide an overall impression of how the performance was received. If your organisation does not currently collect audience feedback, even on an ad-hoc basis, try to do so, you may be surprised at the positive results of such an activity.

Listening to Feedback from Sponsors or Event Organisers

In the same way, it is vital to develop a listening relationship with those organisations that choose to sponsor your event or those that choose to invite you to perform at an event. Supporting an organisation, such as a conductor, is a fantastic thing to do and it is always worth ensuring that the sponsor is included when it comes to making choices regarding music, any accompanying forces etc. so that the person or organisation sponsoring your event feels included. Making sure they feel listened to is the least we can do to acknowledge their generosity.

Likewise, asking questions with those who choose to invite us to perform at events that they are organising helps us listen and understand their expectations: how much music are they expecting?

Are there any specific pieces of music they would like performed? Simple questions but the event organiser will feel included and listened to — all part of being a listening conductor.

Asking for Input

Singers

The time and energy a member gives to singing is always very much valued by those who run the choir and those who musically lead. Good conductors observe their singers' vocal technique and may make recommendations on how to improve their singing. If you lead a community choir, a smaller choir, or a choral society you should expect to be approached, as conductor, for feedback, by any number of singers. Conductors should be only too happy to respond by offering to have a chat or to listen to the choir member singing alone, then offering some feedback that way. Members of a large or symphonic chorus may not always find their conductor is easily accessible but can ask their voice representative for feedback.

Conductors

It is not often that conductors must ask for feedback — it is often forthcoming. However, there may be specific reasons why we might request feedback on something. For example, on how the choir feels about the programming for the upcoming season, whether the balance of sectional rehearsals against full choir rehearsals is correct, whether the upcoming rehearsal schedule is deemed appropriate or a newly tried seating formation in rehearsal is approved. The list could be quite a long one — the key though, is to ask for that input. Managing committees feel much more at ease if they believe that the relationship between the conductor and them is a transparent and communicative one.

On some occasions, I even discussed, with one of my chamber choirs, my thoughts on upcoming tours and concerts and asked for their feedback *en masse*, there and then. However, a lot depends on the nature and tradition of the rehearsal sessions, the size of the choir and whether there is time to take a 'quick show of hands.'

Basic Feedback Chart

Here is a chart of the thought patterns I apply to nearly all feedback. Feedback is important as it encourages communication, but it does not necessarily mean that it will be taken on board and acted upon. Learn to accept that feedback can be used or disregarded as you see fit.

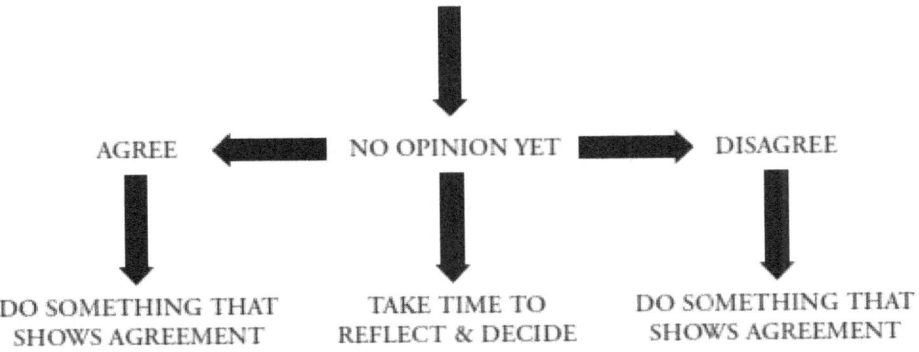

Chapter 15: Listening in a Post-Pandemic World

At the time of writing the world has been irrevocably challenged and changed by the global COVID-19 pandemic. This has meant that entire countries have experienced lockdowns — where the population has been confined to their homes for their health and safety. The world watched as the virus spread, hospitalisations soared and the number of fatal casualties continued to rise. For many, the year 2020 was cancelled; yes the year came and went but as we were all in isolation, it was a year unlike any other. I am writing this in August 2021, in the UK, where most of the restrictions on general life have been lifted, a vaccination programme has been rolled out and we are starting to realise that, somehow, we will have to learn to live with the presence of COVID-19 for the foreseeable future.

The necessary restrictions on our lives over the past 15 months or so have had an unprecedented effect on the arts. Governments have concentrated on keeping economies together but support for the arts has not been a priority, despite its known contribution to health, wellbeing and the economy.

During the pandemic, projected aerosol droplets when singing were considered too much of a danger for singers to be together and so choral singing was stopped specifically. It remained on the list of restrictions well after other restrictions were being lifted and only now, summer 2021, are choirs either returning or planning to return in the autumn. Some choirs were able to return sooner if there was a commercial reason or if they were classed as 'professional'; choirs may well rehearse whilst 'socially distanced', with masks on and with negative COVID-19 tests completed, for some time to come.

During the lockdowns, many choirs took to online platforms to meet, with some retaining rehearsals. Sound latency issues and variable Internet qualities meant that singing together was almost impossible and so singers were confined to singing alone, with their microphones muted; being able to see but not hear others as they rehearsed. Despite the challenges, choirs organised online social or educational events and put together edited video recordings of them singing together. Such is the energy, creativity and passion put into choirs.

Across the arts, many musicians were forced to find alternative careers and some may well choose not to return to their former artistry, so that they can be sure of a steady income in the future ahead.

For singers and choirs, it has been bleak. Some choirs may not survive and some have already ceased. Some singers may not sing publicly again or if they do, it will be 'on weekends only'. The arts world has not just been bruised; it has been damaged. That damage will take a long time to heal, even longer with economies struggling to support national infrastructures and not including the arts in their strategies.

The forced isolation has provided many people with time to think and reflect upon their lives. Time to decide on what the priorities in life are, time to realise that more work than previously thought can be done 'from home', time to decide if a musical career is sustainable or not, time to decide if singing in a choir is taking up too much time or not enough time.

The Effects on Choirs

As we emerge from the restrictions and everyday life begins to resemble what it did before, choirs will begin to meet again for in-person rehearsals. However, long-term isolation without regular rehearsals will have influenced the vocal health and wellbeing of choir members.

Conductors of both amateur and professional singing groups may well find themselves being sought after for advice on the negative effects of the pandemic on singing voices. It is imperative that conductors and vocal coaches know how to respond to this and have information to hand to help guide and support their singers. We must be willing to *listen* to those with concerns or who feel they are struggling. Here are some ailments and concerns singers may have:

- Throat feels dry soon after I start to sing
  I don't seem to have the same breath support that I did before
- My vocal range has diminished — I can't reach the top/bottom register as well as I used to
- I'm struggling to remember the miscellaneous items that were

previously in our repertoire
- I feel tired after singing for about 20–30 minutes
- I keep having to clear my throat all the time
- My voice not sounding very good is making me anxious
- When I could only hear myself, singing whilst online at home, it didn't sound good and I'm not sure I have the confidence to sing again

Scientific findings of the effects of the virus itself on singers, published by international scientific organisations make for comparable reading:

- Lasting respiratory system damage (lungs) including pulmonary legions and lung fibrosis
- Post viral vocal fold paralysis or paresis (intubation can cause this)
- Post viral laryngeal sensory neuropathy (common symptoms chronic cough, swallow dysfunction) – can follow any viral infection
- Chronic fatigue

The important thing to note is that many choirs will have members who have either contracted COVID-19, or who suffer with common ailments because of the lack of regular singing rehearsals. To that end, choirs are going to need sensitive handling when it comes to singing together again. Physical and psychological coaching support — from a musical director or a vocal coach — will be important when choirs resume. Why?

Lack of confidence. Some singers will want to return, and others will only return when they feel it will be safe to do so. Both sets of singers may suffer from a personal lack of confidence in their singing after such a long break

Retraining the muscles. The vocal mechanism is surrounded by a muscular framework. Muscles need regular exercise to remain 'in shape' and our voices should not be thought of as anything different, in this regard

Monitoring for not over singing and over exertion. After a long break it will be tempting for members of our choirs to want to 'blow the cobwebs away' and sing out more than ever; vocal coaches and directors should take care in monitoring that singers warm up properly and should exercise 'listening caution', possibly asking singers to only sing no louder than *mezzo forte* for a while after rehearsals begin and also to keep their eyes open for over use of the supporting muscles in the neck and abdomen, if possible

Re-learning what it is to listen to each other. For some singers it will have been a long time since they have heard their choir sing together live; an opportune moment to discuss blending and the discipline of listening, therefore. Conductors would be wise to address this skill, even early on in newly begun rehearsals.

What am I listening for or what might I observe?

There are several things to listen out for during a rehearsal of your choir, following any long break. However, if your choir has been forced apart because of a pandemic, there is a longer list of 'symptoms' to listen to during the rehearsal itself:

- Singers going red in the face
- Excessive clearing of throats or coughing
- Giving time to get used to following a score and singing
- Inconsistent breathing
- Over-singing
- Individual voices and non-blending
- Emotional response to singing
- Struggling to concentrate for more than 30 minutes
- Vocal tone which is raspy, invariable weak/strong or overly breathy in quality.

How do I manage the symptoms?

It's best to assume that the singers in your choir have not been doing much singing, warm-up exercises or online vocal coaching during a lockdown period. As a result, beginning a new term will be like starting the choir from 'scratch'. This really should be viewed positively; rehearsals can now involve many warm-up exercises designed to carefully warm the voice up and get the 'rusty mechanism moving again more fluidly'.

Take time to listen to the choir as they begin to warm up, observe anyone struggling and chat with them personally later, if possible. Here are some elements to think about when the choir returns after a break:

- Use warm-ups that concentrate on the mid-range of all voice types and gradually expand these to include the lower range first. Then return to the mid-range and progress, step-by-step, to the upper range. Always encourage your singers to stop if they feel uncomfortable
- Start with a single consonant and vowel sound such as 'CAH' or 'SAH' or 'TAH' and gradually work into multiple sounds over a period
- Take care when using warm-ups that cross the *passaggio* and ensure that singers do not try to 'push' too much air through their vocal systems. Instead, ask them to sing in as natural way as possible, even if that means there are some vocal 'clunks' along the way
- Underline the need for engaging with breath support by giving a quick reminder of how breath support works. The key to a solid vocal tone is to run exercises designed to focus on breath support
- Remind singers that despite the break they still belong to the choir. During the exercises, reiterate the need for listening to one another and allowing the voice to 'disappear' into the sound of the whole choir
- Check that the singers shape vowels correctly, engage breath for consonant sounding and sing with intent. Breath with intent is one of the 'casualties' after a long break and needs practice. We take a breath in to sing it out; we don't try and

stop the breath from escaping but use it, as we exhale, to form our vocal tone: in other words, we breathe in ready to sing, we breathe out to sing
- When reading a score and singing is introduced, sing through a significant portion or movement of music beginning to end, regardless of what happens. If the singing 'collapses' and stops as a result, that's OK, encourage the singers to make it to the end of the section or movement — it's a small achievement but a notable one, after a long break
- Take regular breaks, even if that was not the norm previously, so the singers can relax and socialise a little. It will help with their general confidence as they bond once again as a choir.

Listening to a choir sing for the first time after a long break can invoke an emotional response for both singers and the conductor. If you see that some of your singers are visibly moved, allow them space and time to recover. If you are leading the choir and are visibly moved, it's OK to say so. Don't dwell though, ensure your rehearsal keeps moving forward at pace.

New Ideas

Those leading the choir from a management or organisational point of view may have had time to reflect on its standard, development or ambition and will want to talk to about new ideas, initiatives, performances, or processes for the future. View this as a positive move forward and be prepared to listen carefully to what might be suggested. On the other hand, you may have had your own thoughts and ideas for the future and want to be given the opportunity to be listened to, too.

Choirs have had to work hard to survive the pandemic due to the restrictions imposed. Listening to one another, understanding each other and facing the future together will ensure that choirs go from strength to strength.

Who Can I Call upon for Help and Support?

It is crucial not to feel alone, whether we are singing in or leading a choir as we come out of these unprecedented times. So, asking for help is a positive thing.

Fortunately, there are many resources for help and support, here are some of them:

- British Voice Association – http://www.britishvoiceassociation.org.uk
- Making Music – http://www.makingmusic.org.uk
- Sing for Pleasure – http://www.singforpleasure.org.uk
- Association of British Choral Directors – http://www.abcd.org.uk
- Edward-Rhys Harry – http://www.edwardrhysharry.com
- Coro Optimum – http://www.corooptimum.org

Chapter 16: Heart, Soul, and Breath: Listening for Intent

What Do We Mean by Intent?

There is a considerable difference between listening to a choir that understands all that is required to make its performance a successful one and a choir that hopes that it may just be ready enough to put something in front of a listening public.

As conductors we want to look forward to the performances we stage. We want to show the world what we have been working on and, ideally, we want to receive credit and praise for our contribution toward making the performance a successful one. We also want our performances to be as good as possible, so that audiences will support us by coming to our next events.

It is difficult to imagine that any member of a choir cares so little about an impending performance that they do not take personal responsibility for making it successful. Singers directly contribute to the choirs' sound, accuracy and reputation, as well as its confidence. Therefore, they need to put in the work between rehearsals that shows they are familiar with vocal techniques, rehearsal markings, phrasing, breathing and dynamics. More than familiar — practised and part of understanding the music. Choir members put the work in during the rehearsal sessions leading up to a concert to first learn the music and then add the interpretational elements the conductor has envisioned. While preparing for a concert, committed members carefully listen to direction and then respond to it by executing the direction asked for whilst listening to everyone else so that everything can be performed and interpreted together, as a whole.

The members and leader of the choir need to ensure that they are fully ready to perform the music, well before the performance date. Not feeling ready or confident for a concert causes stress and tension, which is easily spread by singers, should they choose to talk to others in the choir about how they feel. There is a powerful psychological reaction if one member of a choir complains that they 'just aren't ready' for a performance, as the curtain rises to a waiting audience — the effect is one of lessening confidence. When singers feel less confident, they are distracted by it. When they are distracted, they lose focus because they start to worry, when they worry, which of the choral disciplines is first to leave? That's right, listening, which in turn can cause public performances to become wan or crumble — because the worry, stress, tension, and distraction of feeling under-confident takes over and, further, then begins to affect the singing as the choir become vocally tense.

When we are fully committed to a performance, when we have rehearsed as much as we can, made all the notes needed in our score, learned our vocal part to within an inch of its life, are familiar with the landscape of all the music so that we can listen to those around us and contribute to the whole… then we'll find freedom. Freedom and confidence to show someone else watching and listening what we want them to see and hear. That freedom from worry or under-confidence empowers us to commit and connect with the music in a way that is rehearsed well and has become familiar. More than familiar, practised. And so, we share our practised art with the world.

When a singer joins a choir or when conductors begin a career directing choirs, the intention is to make music. Making music requires practise. We must learn the music, become more than familiar with it, be able to sing sections from memory because we know it so well, enjoy the freedom of knowing the music we have learned and from within that freedom, show that our intentions are to interpret the music and make it come alive for someone listening. But…

We cannot hope to make it to that golden place of freedom without putting in the work that is needed beforehand. Attending weekly rehearsals is often not enough for singing members. Buying or hiring a copy of the score and listening to a recording once is not enough to prepare if you are a conductor. The key to freedom, confidence and intention in music-making is the preparation and practise.

How can we Identify Singing and Conducting with Intent?

Identifying when a choral piece is either sung or directed with musical intent is not difficult, the signs of intention are relatively clear to all who are listening and observing avidly. Here the signs of a choir singing with musical intent:

- Breathing is rehearsed
- Exhalation is used well, creating solid vocal tone
- Phrasing has all the colours and contours of the required dynamics and uses exhaled breath wholly but without compromise to the ends of phrases, words, or syllables
- First syllables are crisply enunciated against well-shaped and uniform vowels
- All elision is uniform in execution and delivered, in tandem with support from the conductor, by the choir listening to the full shaping of the words and phrases it creates as one organic voice
- Required diphthongs are uniformly placed in the voice
- Any extraneous vocal effects are delivered uniformly section by section
- The choir listens and adapts its overall tone and timbre as it sings, ensuring a blended execution of sound which is consistent across the choir
- Vocal tone is consistent and unwavering at all dynamic levels
- Posture is uniform and at once rehearsed, relaxed and correct for singing
- Singers are not bound to their score, instead they are able to sing through bars and phrases whilst looking directly at the conductor for ensemble direction.

Some of the signs of a conductor directing with intent:

- Physically relaxed but embodies correct posture for singing
- Has 'internalised' the required tempi and beats these clearly without faltering
- Maintains eye contact with the choir
- Glances at the score as necessary but is not bound to it, or conducts from memory
- Does not mouth each word but may shape certain sounds or vowels in the mouth as a visual reminder
- Uses one hand for conducting a beat, the other to direct dynamics as they occur
- May stop conducting in 'beats' to expressively shape phrases and musical contours as rehearsed
- Does not beat either overly expressively or under expressively but embodies the music.

What Stops our Intention to Sing and to Listen?

Much of what stops our intention to sing also stops us from listening and could be reiterated here. Musical intentions can be undermined by a lack of familiarity and knowledge around a piece of music. To show musical intentions, we must be relaxed enough and know exactly what we are doing. So, we must learn, prepare, rehearse, and rehearse again. Our intentions to sing can be stopped by:

- Incorrect posture
- Inadequate breathing preparation
- Uncertainty or poorly expressed consonants, vowels, diction
- Unfamiliarity with the 'landscape' of the score, the music, its structure and design, its vocal parts
- Lack of confidence.

Having our intention to listen stopped can be a separate thing from having our intention to sing stopped. They are different skills, after all. The listening aspect of our rehearsing comes into fruition when we begin to feel freedom from learning notes, allowing us to start thinking of the more expressive qualities of what we are singing. Here are some things that stop singers from listening (in rehearsal or performance):

- Thinking about when to breathe (under rehearsed in this aspect)
- Suddenly remembering previous directions not written down and then doing so mid-sing
- Remembering something to tell the person sitting next to you
- Being on the wrong page
- Hunger/thirst
- Feeling tired
- Outside world distractions
- Trying to decide if we like the music or not
- Being distracted by an audience member
- Being distracted by a choir member

Why Should Singers Listen and Sing with Intent?

Listening for the sake of listening is of little value as it does not presuppose a linked action. Listening with the intention of singing using the advice and guidance of a conductor, however, brings action to your listening — an outworking of the listening and, therefore, fruit of your labour. If all members of a choir fully listened with intent, the work of a conductor would be made very much easier. However, that intention to listen, to work out an action or direction, is not always consistent. We all have lives that can distract, thoughts and reflections that can get in the way, singing neighbours to chat to sociably — the list goes on. Needless to say, the choir that listens with intent gleans the most information from its rehearsal process, learns deeper about its own singing and sound and is more well-rounded, musically speaking. We should listen with intent to be musically better — surely one of our intentions when joining a choir?

The Three Principles of Embodiment: Heart, Soul, Breath

When singers have listened to direction, rehearsals, and vocal lines enough to begin to find the freedom in singing with musical intention, they can begin to embody the music they are singing. In other words, they can express themselves not only through the vocal mechanism but through their whole bodies connecting with the music. This embodiment of music — the deeper connection found through listening, learning, and finding the freedom to express with intention — carries with it a proven ability to better our sense of wellbeing. In short, the commitment we attach to listening will better our musical experiences and reap benefits for our sense of wellness physically and mentally.

Jacques Launay is a researcher in experimental psychology at the University of Oxford. In his online article about choral singing and wellbeing, he says, *"…the physiological benefits of singing, and music more generally, have long been explored. Music making exercises the brain as well as the body, but singing is particularly beneficial for improving breathing, posture, and muscle tension. Listening to and participating in music has been shown to be effective in pain relief, too, probably due to the release of neurochemicals such as □ -endorphin (a natural painkiller responsible for the "high" experienced after intense exercise)."*[4]

I would add that the physical and mental wellbeing of a choral singer is further positively affected when the singing is combined with listening with intention and the outworking of those intentions bringing the success sought.

To gain the success hoped for as a choral singer of any type of choir, the intentions of a singer's heart and mind must be consistent, even from the first breath of their rehearsal. They should:

- Have the intention of success in their heart and mind
- Listen and listen until they understand the music and the directions asked for and their voice becomes part of the whole

---

[4] Launay (2015) https://bit.ly/3LbeAk7 (accessed Feb 2022)

- Find freedom of expression through listening to direction and to the whole choir
- Experience wellbeing in their soul from their success
- Breathe in to breathe out, listen and make music.

Matching Intent with Direction

Directing choirs is all about intent. In whichever way a choir is directed, it must be with clear intent. That intent comes from:

- Adequate preparation of scores
- Knowing what to listen for to fix things
- Having the intention of aiding the singers in connecting with the music
- Having a clear and structured approach to learning and rehearsing the music
- Directing with clarity of beat
- Ensuring the relationship between dynamics in the music is listened to, explored and settled
- Knowing the music, including each vocal part or being able to instant sing it
- Building confidence in the choir by knowing what you want and achieving it through a well-planned rehearsal schedule published in advance

Directors should embody the performance directions in the score where appropriate and remain connected to the music; this in turn will be mirrored by the choir when they find their freedom point. Beating should not be compromised and rehearsing the beating of a piece whilst balancing expression with gesture is vital, so do not be afraid of rehearsing for hours in front of a mirror. The basis of all of this is listening to the music as it develops and understanding the musical intentions of the composer so that those intentions may be translated adequately into conducting gesture.

A Note about the Intent of Your Breath

Breath is life. Good breathing whilst singing can aid wellbeing. A singer's in breath brings oxygen but they need to exhale to take in a new breath. Whilst learning music, a singer's breathing becomes compromised; they learn not to use the fullness of their breath, to under sing or to 'mark' their way through sections of music as they try to learn it. In fact, the way a piece is rehearsed can differ in many ways, according to the singer's breathing. It is important therefore that when they are learning or rehearsing music with the whole choir that the singers breathe together and use the fullness of their breath – together. That breathing becomes uniform and 'in sync'. Then they must fight against trying to hold on to their breath in any way and learn how to utilise the breath better: only by relaxing and allowing the breath out of their bodies can they learn how to manage its inhalation and exhalation. We must not try to influence their breath by trying to hold on to it or stop it escaping as they sing, for this inhibits the natural rhythm to their breathing; it is that rhythm of inhalation and exhalation that helps singers to sing together – in rhythm. It is that rhythm to their breathing that helps singers with the intention of each breath and it is that intention of each breath that they should hear in their friends and colleagues in a choir. If they can hear it, they can listen for it and if they listen for it they can do it as one. And who will lead this living, listening, breathing organism of human musicality? The person who has helped shape each rehearsal moment and each performance: the listening conductor.

Chapter 17. Connections

Sometimes, the work one puts into directing choirs can have the most unexpected effects.

At a concert performance I was directing in North East Wales, UK, one dark and dreary February, the choir, with whom I had been working for about 18 months, crossed a line. They had been working hard, at developing their sense of performance and had had cause, amongst themselves, as members, to reflect on their *raison d'etre*; why they existed and how to be as good as possible at it. I had spent some time simply listening to them sing and had begun work, in earnest, in the rehearsal room, impressing upon them how they might connect (even) further with their music making. The basic sound they made was good and I had been determined to push this choir forward into becoming even more accomplished.

The first half of this particular concert (a miscellaneous programme of music from the classical era to the present day) had gone well and I had noticed that the choir were no longer just singing, that instead, many members knew their parts so well that they were singing with a freedom that vanquished the stress and tension - which can affect singers in any amateur choir - and allowed them to listen freely to one another as well as freely follow some spontaneous direction of the pieces, as I connected with their new-found freedom, sound and breathing. The first half ended with rapturous applause, and I returned to my dressing room to focus on the 'second half.'

There came a knock on my door and, on autopilot, "come in", I responded. The door burst open, and 3 gentlemen of the bass section came bounding in, throwing their arms around me and two of them with actual tears.

'Thank you, thank you, thank you' they cried, shaking my hands, patting me on the back. "Thank you so much for all that you are doing with this choir — we sound so different now, we've been listening to what you've been saying, and we can hear the difference right across the choir. Please keep going and push us even harder to develop, will you?".

They were so excited and so full of energy that I could not help but respond to their requests to keep going, and the second half of the concert was as good as the first. One of those gentlemen was highly esteemed in his own world of work, with an enviable and justifiable international reputation. The choir noted that day that they had indeed started to develop. As a result of this acknowledgement, they continued to work hard at their musicality in performance and gained much in the way of reputation and membership recruitment.

Why am I sharing this memory with you? The reason is simple; listening creates the opportunity to hear. And hearing creates the opportunity to connect. The more you listen, the more you hear, the more you connect, creatively, with what you hear.

As conductors we can spend much of our time being preoccupied with how *we* want to direct passages of music but how aware are we of that natural, organic process of listening, hearing, and responding to the singers before us? Do we allow pre-planning the direction of a piece of music to quash a better performance by an ensemble because we choose to do what *we* want to do and not what might be best musically for the ensemble before us? And how conscious are we of our own connection to the music — and how it affects what we are listening to and what we hear?

As choral conductors, we should consider ourselves a conduit, a vessel, if you like, for helping others to create music of the most human kind — with their voices.

The very nature of choral singing is personal. The members of a choir have joined it because they enjoy singing together; they enjoy hearing the result of their hard work and preparation culminating in a (often) public showing of the fruits of their labour: all choirs hope to perform to and please an audience. They also hope to please their conductor.

As conductors, do we hope to please our choirs? Do we know how to please our choirs?

There is no better way to lead rehearsals of a choral kind than to act as a facilitator of music making for those present with humility and servitude: egocentric leaders have short or shallow careers and develop reputations that do not inspire envy. Someone must lead, yes: that person, in their wisdom, will want to provide the very best experience for their singers that they can. Boastful arrogance and "I'm in charge" syndrome may conjure up fear, but we should not operate in this way. Instead, our leadership should show through careful preparation, understanding, knowledge of the music and its context and treating our singers with the respect they deserve as willing partakers in music creation of this kind.

The Conductor's Connection

One of the major routes to aiding a choir in its development is for its conductor to be unafraid of showing their own human connection to music making in this way. Why? The short answer is that our own energy and enthusiasm for the music will inspire those who sing in our choirs to learn and develop along with us. Conductors are only able to feel comfortable in displaying a connection to the music *when they know it*. When they know it so well that they can 'inhabit' the music. Perhaps inhabiting the music is not the best expression – a better way of describing it might be that the conductor knows the music so well that it almost becomes a part of them – and therefore they are able to 'embody' the music – bringing the expression of the music into the conductors' body and gestural language, as a way of direction.

There is a clear process that conductors will go through to prepare themselves for directing a piece of music. In short this process is:

- Listening to the piece
- Listening to the piece whilst following with the score
- Learning the voice parts
- Learning the accompaniment (either physically or theoretically)
- Learning the piece well enough to 'hear' it without the aid of a recording
- Transitioning from listening and learning, via revision, to knowing the piece and understanding its layout, design, and structure
- Dependent on length and complexity, being able to hear the piece and conduct it through from memory, accurately
- Having developed confidence by listening, learning, and now knowing the piece, becoming 'free' of the learning to add personal interpretation to the direction of the piece
- Having achieved all the above, be freely willing to adapt personal interpretation to the group of singers in a rehearsal room as you listen to the piece develop

- To get the best out of the singers, according to ability, be willing to compromise — or be inspired to further develop — personal interpretation through listening to the rehearsals

Look at how the words 'listen' and 'hear' appear in the process listed above. The connection between listening to the music which we must prepare and then hearing the cause and effect of learning within the choral rehearsal are intrinsically linked: we cannot hope to aid our choirs in helping to fix, modify, strengthen confidence and encourage artistry – at any level - unless we have already trodden that same path and have arrived at the point where we are artistically fully prepared to direct a concert performance of the music even before the first hour of rehearsal for it. Then we are ready to give direction of a piece of music with contextual understanding, historical authenticity where necessary, a full knowledge of the 'musical landscape' of the work(s) and composer(s) and above all an artistic integrity worthy of someone in musical leadership, whether in an amateur or professional capacity. The integrity of our role as a musical leader is always in the balance the moment we step on to the rehearsal podium or up to the rehearsal music stand; when we stand there and begin our rehearsals we are representing not only our own musicianship but that of our colleagues nationally and internationally who are all doing the same.

Our preparation gives us freedom to lift the music 'from the page to the stage' and means we are in the position where we are not distracted by following lines on a page, with our heads constantly stuck in a score as we rehearse, checking for any mistakes we *may* have heard. Instead, we have the freedom to look at and engage with our singers face to face, to really listen to them sing, to acknowledge and encourage their efforts -whilst listening - and to feedback with accuracy and reliability; to develop a sound working relationship with them built on the knowledge gained from our own preparation, which in turn should inspire confidence in our singers that we know what we hope to achieve – and how to get it in a fun, energised, musical, non-autocratic way. In other words, we have done and are doing our job. Listening is one of the key elements of our job and we need to be free from the page enough to engage fully with it.

The other gain, in freedom from the page, is that we are free to interpret: to develop and rehearse our gestural language, expression and artistry as we direct.

Rehearsals are not just for our singers; they are an important opportunity for us as conductors to experiment with or overlay our intended gestural language and expression in a work(s) and then rehearse this with our singers. This, of course, may change as we work with and listen to our singers. As the singers become more familiar with our gesture and expression, the more they see the humanity in our own music making; the more humanity and expression they see, the stronger the bond of understanding between choir and conductor becomes — a proper connection. The stronger the connection, the stronger the confidence, the stronger the confidence, the stronger the artistry and musicianship.

About Public Performances

Listening is the core of what enables conductors of vocal ensembles to do their work. That listening should be combined with adequate score preparation before a rehearsal, is a must for effective rehearsals, performances, and conductors.

Vocal ensembles of all kinds prepare music they want to share with the outside world. They hope to perform the music they have diligently prepared, for a public, whether paying or not.

Performances of music should be well rehearsed before being made public and so should the directorial gestures and beating that go with creating those performances. Conductors should though, take a great deal of care to ensure that they remain *listening intently* during the public performances they are directing. The distraction of an audience or the rush of adrenaline that can happen with public singing are two very clear reasons why singers can stop listening to the ensemble or themselves or their sections. The discipline of the listening choir is tested to its limit when that choir is performing in public: the one person who must not allow compromise of that listening, at any cost, is the conductor, for that is where the eyes and ears of the singers will be should they begin to sense something has gone awry.

The listening choir is in the best position when it has the listening conductor to help guide it.

Connecting In Performance

Performances can produce the most magical, moving and inspirational moments for a choir, but how do we, as conductors, engage with our singing ensembles effectively, during performances, to facilitate these 'magical moments'?

Conducting choirs in public is different to coaching and helping to develop them in the rehearsal room. A conductor will lead their choir through public performances unable to 'fix' things, rehearse things or change things as the choir presents its rehearsed material before an audience.

During the rehearsal period we have listened as the choir has learned new notes and phrases, as well as linguistic and expressionistic nuances to help with the delivery of the text and musical framework; we have listened for inconsistency of vocal tone and timbre, stray consonant placing, changes in intonation and lack of clarity in diction and we have listened as the choir's sense of ensemble has developed alongside its confidence.

During a performance, we must continue to listen. Our work is not done until the end of the silence after a performance(s).

Here are some suggested reasons as to why we should continue to listen during performances:

- Listen to check if the choir has taken a good preparatory breath (and will, therefore, be accurately on time for their first entry)
- Listen to identify if the choir can hear its accompanying forces well and/or properly
- Listen for any changes in the voice sections due to them performing in public – do some voices sound quieter? Louder? Do some sections suddenly sound with an 'uneven' blend? Why? Can something be done using gestural language to try to even the blend out?
- Listen for any changes of sound produced by the acoustic of the performance venue – are some voices magnified as a result? Do some phrases need to be given space to 'sound' in an acoustic with a generous reverberation? Would some voice sections sound better seated differently in this particular performance venue?

- Listen for changes in textual clarity
- Listen for sudden losses in confidence or ensemble and be ready to guide voice sections back to confidence through the language of your conducting
- Listen for changes in the choir's perception of its own dynamics and adjust accordingly using gesture
- Listen to the relationship between your beating pattern and the amount of breath available in your singers; do they correspond? Are you beating slower than the amount of breath they have available collectively in each phrase? Are you beating with too much breath available? How does the volume of breath available within your beating (tempo) alter the delivery of the choir's dynamics, tone, posture, focus and clarity of diction? Is your conducting pattern connected with your choir's inhalation and exhalation? And has the volume of breath you perceive as available become different from rehearsal mode to performance mode?
- If you are also directing an accompanying instrumental ensemble, listen for how well the relationship between the singer's and instrument's phrasing and dynamics is working and respond accordingly with gesture and direction – also check if the agreed balances created in the rehearsal are still correct or appropriate with the presence of an audience in the room

These are just some suggestions of how our listening might continue during performances, but the point here is that without listening we are not truly taking part in a performance, we are merely bystanders. Those whom we are leading are dependent on our continued listening and with practice we may begin to listen well enough to predict if something will go awry or if new spontaneous ways of direction might be successful. And we cannot truly listen if we are distracted by the score; the score is useful should we have a moment of forgetfulness or are unsure about something suddenly: the true freedom to listen comes from knowing the work without the need to look at the score too much and therefore engage more fully with the act of performance.

Chapter 18: In a Nutshell

Listening: A Discipline

The chapters of this book have been woven together by one underlying aim: to stress the importance listening plays in the activity, discipline and semi-societal makeup of a group of individuals who sing together.

I have referred to such groups as vocal ensembles, singing groups and as a choir, as a reminder that the discipline of listening should be treated as equally worthy of a barbershop chorus, a quartet, a chamber choir, a cambiata, a symphonic chorus, an LGBTQ+ choir, a male voice choir, a female voice choir, a youth choir or just about any other vocal ensemble you can imagine. It is the one discipline that is required of all these singers and their conductors, to make music together, successfully.

Sadly, it can be the one discipline that is often neglected or not coached, in choral rehearsals; it can be the one discipline that a conductor does not use in their preparation and rehearsal; the one aspect of a performance that disappears under the pressure of being listened to by a public audience and the one aspect that can be upset by the acoustic or formation of a singing ensemble, at a concert venue.

Like all disciplines, listening can be taught, coached, reminded about, practised and developed to a high standard. Like any discipline, listening is required to be a consistent feature of rehearsals, a consistent feature of a choral leader's toolkit, a consistent feature in performance. Being inconsistent with this most sensitive of disciplines, results in inconsistent results in both rehearsals and public performances.

Let's consider the commitment needed to become an athlete competing at either a high amateur, or semi-professional or fully professional standard in competition: at the beginning of their development, an athlete will be trained by a coach to achieve the best possible results in a local competition, then maybe a county competition, then perhaps a regional competition and on to a country-wide competition. There are distinct levels in which an athlete may compete. If their results are proven to equal or higher than those of their competing colleagues, the athlete may receive an invitation to compete at a higher level and so on. To be good enough, an athlete understands that they must work hard, starting their training in informal athletic training and developing their skills through commitment and dedication to their sport on a very regular basis, refining their abilities and physical understanding of their sport through disciplined practise — rehearsals for competitions.

As directors of a choir, it is important that we understand that there is a set of skills we can develop as individuals and as an ensemble, when singing; the quality of those skills may be refined as much as we commit to refining them; ask yourself the question, 'am I committed to being the best at my singing, or leading, that I can?' The answer should be yes!

Therefore, we should embrace the fact that listening is one of the core disciplines necessary to accomplish the goal of being better at ensemble singing, or leading. And we can accomplish a higher standard of music making by committing to being as disciplined as possible in our listening.

Listening: A Practised Art

As previously discussed, listening might be considered a 'practised art'; it is certainly a skill, at the very least. I mentioned, in chapter 3, that listening can be both a personal and group activity. In fact, both aspects of listening – personal and public if you like – are required to be practised and developed over time and as familiarity with the music becomes recognised.

I don't pretend that listening whilst singing or conducting, simultaneously, is an easy skill to develop. It's not, but it does require consistency in order to be developed. Perhaps the best way to start on the journey of better listening is to use a commercial recording and a copy of the written music together: sit and follow the music score through whilst listening to the recording and then listen again whilst singing the vocal parts. The advantage here is you can make it somewhat easier for yourself by turning up the volume of the speakers or headphones as you sing. As a reminder from the beginning of this book, our ears are not well designed for listening to ourselves and others simultaneously, hence the need to train ourselves! But this listening training is also a rehearsal for being in the same room as live singers and develops within us a deeper familiarity of vocal lines, making it easier to identify aurally and then listen to them as we sing.

The one thing to remember, though, is that we can practise and we should practise. We should practise because we want to better ourselves in our choral singing, whether we are a member of the local amateur operatic society or sing with a city symphonic chorus. We should want to be a valued leader of the vocal ensemble that we lead and developing our listening skills through practice is one worthy way of being able to contribute well.

Listening: A Necessity

Developing and refining our listening skills is a necessity. When we join a vocal ensemble of one kind or another, we join (possibly) an established group of singers. By joining them, (through audition or not) we hope to be welcomed, accepted and add enrichment to our lives; this can be said for both amateur and professional singers. The one thing we should be aiming for is to add our contribution to the singing group in a positive way, as a conductor. It is a necessity, therefore, that part of our contribution is listening to all instructions, listening to our friends and colleagues and to allow our listening to inform the way we blend our own voice (or direction) into the established qualities of the group.

Joining a group and then not listening to that group would be disastrous. Singers don't join singing groups to prove a point, have their voices stick out 'like a sore thumb', show others 'how it is done' elsewhere or because they want to be noticed.

They join, as a singer, to enhance the sound, blend and standard of the group. We join, as a conductor, to help shape and direct that sound.

As a necessary discipline in choral singing, listening is tantamount to 'joining the ranks' of the other singers and becoming a part of them. In smaller choirs or ensembles, each individual voice is crucial — and therefore each ear that listens are equally as crucial. The same can be said for each voice in each voice section of a larger choir. The crucial quality is listening and blending to enhance the sound. Listening is therefore of necessity to each choral singer and conductor.

Listening: A Courtesy

Just as listening is a discipline, practicable and a necessity, it is also a courtesy. It is not often that 'choral manners' are discussed, either in a rehearsal or a performance, however we should remember that singing together means that singers devote their time to a hobby or career that involves other human beings. It would therefore be sensible to argue that for a rehearsal to be successful, they must listen to the instructions or direction given by the leader or conductor; that they listen and take note by writing reminders in their score or an accompanying note pad. That courtesy of listening to the person who has prepared for the rehearsal beforehand and is responding to the singing after listening to it, as well as conducting or leading it, should be extended to fellow singers in the ensemble by listening to the overall sound the group makes, listening to the voice section they belong to, listening to those sat or stood near them, listening to any accompanying instrument. It is courteous to listen so that we are sensitive to the sound around us and therefore do our best to become a part of the creation of that sound unobtrusively. It is courteous to listen in order to learn or be reminded about the vocal qualities needed for dynamics and interpretation, uniform breathing and diction, phrasing, tempo changes. In short, listening is a courtesy that we must afford our colleagues to make the choir work.

Listening: A Tool

Finally, listening is the tool we use to get the job done, whether we sing or conduct or both. It is the tool that we can all use to ensure that ensemble singing is successful, it is the common tool between us in order that we might share and listen to feedback, it is the tool that should be most used to 'fix things' and make them better, to identify areas of weakness and then address them, to understand and execute vocal blend, mix and match voice types, find vocal zones, assess the qualities of dynamics and other vocal effects and to assess and ascertain the overall vocal standards to which we all aspire.

It is the tool in the kitbag of any singer or conductor that sets them aside as sensitive, courteous, understanding, able to react and respond, aid, worthy of trust and above all, a music maker of aspiring standards. Whatever type of chorus you direct, make listening your priority.

Be The Listening Conductor.

Resources

THE LISTENING CONDUCTOR – *THE PODCAST*

Hosted by author Edward-Rhys Harry, this companion to the book *THE LISTENING CONDUCTOR*, has in depth interviews and discussion on choral conducting technique with guests including Simon Halsey, Neil Ferris, Sarah Mc Donald, Sofi Jeannin, Ken Burton and others. Available now at AUDIBLE and most other podcast platforms.

    Twitter: @TLConductor
    Instagram: the listening conductor
    Facebook: https://www.facebook.com/The-Listening-Conductor-102429489062153
    Email: thelisteningconductor@gmail.com

CORO OPTIMUM LTD.

An organisation created for the training and development of choral conductors today. Mentor schemes, conducting technique training days, 24/7 helpline, score study and preparation days, specialist days for those working in education (all levels) and support and entry into diploma qualifications in music direction.

    www.corooptimum.org

THE HARRY ENSEMBLE LTD.

A chamber choir based in the South of England, specialises in performing the music of established and contemporary composers of the UK by performing overseas every season. Also runs a successful and competitive Assistant Conductor Training Scheme with applications open all year round.

    www.harryensemble.com

EDWARD-RHYS HARRY

    Author, podcast host, choral clinician, and consultant.
    www.edwardrhysharry.com

Bibliography

"listen." *Merriam-Webster.com*. 2021. https://www.merriam-webster.com (8 August 2011).

E. Gould, *Behind Bars*, London: Faber Music Ltd., 2011

J. Grier, *The Critical Editing of Music*, Cambridge: Cambridge University Press, 1996

Hollins/Vango, How To Make Your Choir Sound Awesome, York, Banks Music Publishing, 2022

Launay (2015) https://bit.ly/3LbeAk7 (accessed Feb 2022)

Mussulrian, J.A. Dear People: Robert Shaw, A Biography. Indiana University Press, 1979

Ravall, Sofie: Logopedics, Master's Thesis, Åbo Akademi University, Finland, 2015

www.ingramcontent.com/pod-product-compliance
Lightning Source LLC
Chambersburg PA
CBHW051054160426
43193CB00010B/1184